Getting More Done

10 Steps for Outperforming Busy People

Chris Crouch

Nyack Library
59 South Broadway
Nyack, NY 10960-3834

GETTING MORE DONE.
Copyright © 2010 by Chris Crouch.

All rights reserved.
No part of this book may be used or reproduced in any manner without written permission except for brief quotations in articles or reviews. Proper credit required.

Requests for permission should be addressed to:

Dawson Publishing
3410 S. Tournament Drive
Memphis, TN 38125

Printed in the United States of America.

Cover design: Tart Design

For information on quantity discounts for bulk purchases, special sales or use in corporate training programs, please contact Dawson Publishing at 901.494.3673 or rthomas@dawsonpublishing.com.

ISBN-13: 978-0-97586806-5

2010935226

Also by Chris Crouch

Happiness
Simple Ideas to Help Create a Better Life

Licking Your Elbow
Cures for Craziness at Work

Being Productive
Learning How to Get More Done with Less Effort

Getting Organized
Improving Focus, Organization, and Productivity

The Contented Achiever
How to Get What You Want and Love What You Get
(with Don Hutson and George Lucas)

Simple Works
Simple Ideas to Make Life Better
(with Susan Drake)

Skipping the Traditional Long Introduction

This book is small by design. Busy people do not have time for cluttered writing and complexity, so I'll keep things short and simple. We'll be in pretty good intellectual company since Einstein once said, "Make everything as simple as possible, but not simpler."

I want to help you become more grounded, centered, and focused on what's important, so you can be successful ... or more successful.

This book is about turning things around, replacing frantic motion with constructive action, being highly productive, and creating the joyful and balanced lifestyle we all hear so much about.

We'll stick with the big issues. I won't try to solve world hunger, so to speak, with this little book. I'll just take you through 10 easy-to-understand and easy-to-implement steps to help you realize more of your potential and enjoy work more.

If You've Read My Other Books ...

There are many similarities, and many differences, between this book and my other books. Two of my previous books, *Getting Organized* and *Being Productive*, present a lot of ideas in a buffet-type format – the reader chooses ideas they want to try and decides on the order of implementation. Since I'm not a big believer in any sort of one-size-fits-all solution, this seemed like a good way to share ideas. But since writing these books, I've had requests for a specific plan to become more focused, organized, and productive, including the suggested order of implementation. So, I'm taking a position on how to get the job done in this book. If you've read my other books, you'll recognize a few ideas, but there are many new ideas and more specifics on implementation.

So here it is. My suggestions on how to get the job done once and for all ... 10 specific steps, implemented in order, preferably over a 10-day period – steps that will absolutely turn things around for you and get you on a highly focused, highly productive, highly organized, highly enjoyable path in life. I wish you much success!

Contents

1	Slow Down, Pause, and Reset	9
2	Establishing and Maintaining an Always Follow-Up Reputation	25
3	Finding Things Quickly When You Need Them	45
4	Absolutely Ruthless E-mail Management	57
5	Managing Meeting Mania	67
6	Goldilocks Planning	81
7	The Art and Science of Persuading	93
8	Leveraging Your Time Through Networking	101
9	Busy Tapes	113
10	Following Through	123

| 1

Slow Down, Pause, and Reset

First Things First …
The Beginning of the End of Chaos

When stress is high, it is difficult to solve any problems. Dealing with the stress – more specifically, doing something to lower it – is almost always the first problem that must be solved. Yes, in most situations, stress reduction comes before you make any attempt to solve other problems. And surprisingly, if you lower stress, other problems often disappear without further effort on your part.

I learned this many years ago in a customer service course. When dealing with an upset customer, the first priority is reducing stress and tension so everyone can begin thinking clearly. It's better to work on the customer's stated problem after everyone is in a reasonably calm state of mind. This strategy works when dealing with upset customers, and it works when dealing with an out-of-control work life.

A Racecar without a Steering Wheel

Before getting into specific techniques, let's talk about stress and your brain.

- Parts of your brain are designed to help you react and respond quickly and automatically (without thinking) to threatening or potentially dangerous situations.

- Other areas of your brain are designed to evaluate your situation, make behavioral adjustments, and steer you in the right direction. These areas control your higher-order cognitive processes and help you think, plan, compare, analyze, organize, and control impulsive behavior.

Excessive stress shuts down or significantly inhibits these higher-order cognitive functions and places the reactive-responsive areas of your brain in charge of your behavior. In a nutshell, excessive stress makes you react and respond without thinking much about it. Under too much stress, you become like a racecar without a steering wheel. That's the major problem with excessive busyness and the accompanying stress it usually generates – it prevents you from thinking, planning, comparing, analyzing, organizing, and controlling impulsive behavior.

A typical outcome of too much stress is an inability to control your impulses to check e-mails, text messages, Facebook, Twitter, and so on, even when you know you have much more important things to do. You, in effect, train your nervous system (the ultimate controller of your behavior) to operate in this manner on an ongoing basis. This becomes your default mode of behavior. In other words, in the absence of anything to prevent you from doing it, you default to behavior that severely diminishes your sound judgment and productivity.

The Components of the Solution

Okay, so you want to change your default behavior. How can you go about doing this? It takes three things: a design solution, appropriate emotional awareness, and repetition.

The design solution idea comes from Buckminster Fuller, an early 1900s designer, inventor, and futurist. Fuller said,

> "The function of what I call design science is to solve problems by introducing into the environment new artifacts, the availability of which will induce their spontaneous employment by humans and thus, coincidentally, cause humans to abandon their previous problem-producing behavior and devices. For example, when humans have a vital need to cross the roaring rapids of a river, as a design scientist I would design them a bridge,

causing them, I am sure, to abandon spontaneously and forever the risking of their lives by trying to swim to the other shore."

Imagine that for years, people have tried to determine a good way to get across the roaring rapids of a river. They've tried swimming across, rafting across, canoeing across, and many other methods. In general, everything they have tried is dangerous, difficult, and less than effective. Then one day, an engineering-minded individual introduces a new artifact into the environment – a bridge. Now they have a choice. If they want to get to the other side of the river, what do you think most of them will do? Yep, they'll use the bridge.

The bridge is an example of a design solution – a structure or structured process that helps solve an ongoing problem or effectively deals with issues placing limitations on potential success. Ultimately, we need a design solution to cross over the hours of our chaotic workdays.

We also need an emotional component to our solution. There are basically two ways to alter behavior: attach some extreme negative emotion or unpleasant physical sensation to the performance of the existing behavior, or attach positive emotions or physical sensations to the performance of the desired behavior. Let's say you believe it is an acceptable idea to unhesitatingly touch a hot stove. You can easily change this behavior by actually touching a hot stove. This will likely attach an extreme physical sensation to the old behavior and alter your behavior from that point in time forward.

In general, positively reinforcing new behavior is more practical and feasible in most work-life situations. Here's how it works: The brain and other components of your nervous system possess a characteristic called neuroplasticity. This means your brain is highly malleable – it can be changed. For example, when certain brain cells "light up" or are activated, they might set neurological events in motion causing you to check your e-mail. Another group of brain cells might instruct you to work on your most important priority for the day. Yet another group might cause you to get hungry and go to lunch ... and so forth and so on. Therefore, patterns of activated brain cells determine behavior. A distinct combination of activated brain cells exists for every action you take. As you repeatedly activate certain groups of cells, you reinforce the resulting default or comfort-zone behavior. Continue activating a certain group of cells repetitively and you develop what we commonly refer to as a habit.

If you think of behavior production this way, the process for changing behavior is fairly straightforward. Neuroplasticity, the biological process that produces behavior change, is primarily driven by repetition. Find a way to spend more time activating groups of cells that produce desired behavior and less time activating groups of cells that produce undesired behavior. In short, set up a design process that strongly encourages you to replace undesired behavior with desired behavior.

Think about it, all of these internal brain processes can work for or against you. It's simple: Good habits work for you and bad habits work against you. Let's explore ways to create habits that work for you. Let's develop a design solution to help you create highly productive behavior and figure out a way to repeat the use of the design solution until neuroplasticity "does its thing" and creates new habits.

Yes, There Are Limits to Life ... and a Workday

As a human, especially if you consider yourself a high-achieving human, it's not fun or fashionable to think of your limitations. However, among a group of people, the most successful person is usually the person whose beliefs correspond most closely with reality. Here's a stark example of reality: You cannot pour a gallon into a quart jar and you cannot plan to do more than 86,400 seconds worth of activity in a day ... including work, sleep, rest, recreation, and so on. There are limits to what anyone, including me and you, can do in a day. And that's okay. It's a good idea to accept. You are not a bad or lazy person if you accept the premise that there are limits to what you can and should take on at work.

At some point in time, employers decided that eight hours constituted a typical workday. Maybe that's a good number, maybe not. Let's say for now that an eight-hour day appears reasonable. Once you implement the ideas in this book, you can adjust that number up or down based on the results you are getting and what your body is telling you in terms of stress and anxiety. For now, let's make our goal calling it quits most days after eight hours.

The Turnaround

In order to initiate the turnaround from frantic motion to productive action, start by putting a reasonable limit on what you designate as important during a given period of time, in this case, an eight-hour workday.

Let's think very short-term to initiate the turnaround process. In the long run, I believe in maintaining a long-term vision supported by a short-term focus on activities that support the vision. However, when your "todays" are out of control, you might want to think more like an emergency room triage physician and focus mainly on short-term critical activities to get things quickly under control. We'll talk more about long-term issues later; it's not time to think about what you want to do with the rest of your life when you are not sure how you are going to make it through today. Remember, you've got to take some action to get those higher-order functions of your brain reengaged before tackling long-term strategic and tactical issues. Once your nervous system and stress-inducing habits are under control, you can relax and focus more on your long-term vision of success.

Broken Windows in Reverse

In his book, *The Tipping Point*, Malcolm Gladwell explains the broken windows theory. Say a factory building is abandoned in an area near your neighborhood. As long as the building remains in pretty good condition, everything is fine. But suppose someone comes along and throws a rock and breaks a window. If the window is quickly repaired, everything still remains fine. However, if the window is not promptly repaired, it sends a message to potential vandals that nobody is watching and nobody cares. So another window is broken, and another, and another. In a short period of time, the vandalism escalates, the building is destroyed, and then the vandalism creeps to other areas adjacent to the building. Eventually, the tipping point is reached and the entire area deteriorates and becomes an undesirable place to work or live. According to the broken windows theory, the spreading problem could have been prevented by taking a simple action – fixing the first broken window. So, contrary to what you sometimes hear, it is often a good idea to sweat the small stuff.

But let's reverse the broken windows theory. Let's assume that the chaos, in this case the chaos in your work life instead of your neighborhood, has already passed the tipping point and spread. Why not find some simple action to take, like fixing a broken window, to reverse the process and begin turning things around? According to the case studies mentioned in Gladwell's book, including ones about significantly reducing crime in New York City, this strategy works quite well.

The 3x5 Design Solution

Considering all I have said so far, let's talk about a simple design solution you can easily repeat to get a new group of highly productive brain cells firing and driving sound planning and prioritizing habits.

1   Get a package of 3x5 index cards. They usually come in packs of 100.

2   Get a marking pen, preferably a felt tip or Sharpie-type pen that creates bold letters or script. However, any pen will work.

3   Open the package and put 90 of the index cards aside. We'll use some of them later.

4   Make a commitment to the following: At least until I get things under control, I am going to put a reasonable limit on the quantity of important activities I attempt to pack into my work schedule. Until further notice, that limit is no more than 10 items at a time. At any point in time, if I decide to add activities, that's fine – as long as I eliminate an equal number of existing activities. Less than 10 important activities is okay. More than 10 is unacceptable if I want to get rid of my stress-inducing work overload.

5   Next, in words, acronyms, diagrams, sketches, or anything you will clearly understand later today, tomorrow, and for the next few days, document the

10 most important activities you believe you need to focus on tomorrow – 10 activities on 10 cards, one activity per card. For example, I have a card in my current stack that simply says "SS4W." That means working on a posting for my SmartStuff4Work blog (www.smartstuff4work.com) is currently a high-priority activity for me. It's one of my 10.

6   Spread all 10 index cards face up on your desk. Pick the card representing your highest priority (in your subjective opinion) and turn it face down on your desk. Repeat the process with your next highest priority, and so forth and so on, until all 10 cards are in a single stack face down on your desk. Turn the entire stack over and congratulate yourself on efficiently and effectively planning and prioritizing your workload for the next day.

7   Make a commitment to get closure on, or make significant progress on, the top three priorities each day ... and at least try to nudge forward or make some progress on the other seven items. Define success as making any sort of significant progress on the top three priorities, which can of course change from day to day. If you get anything else done in a given day, consider it a bonus.

8   Allocate a minimum of 32 minutes to each of your top three priorities each day. Use a timer. Set it for 32 minutes and stay totally focused on the task at

hand until the timer goes off – no interruptions … no exceptions!

9   Begin working on your No. 1 priority no later than 10 a.m., your No. 2 priority no later than 2 p.m., and your No. 3 priority no later than 4 p.m.

10 Repeat this process every workday … forever!

You now have three choices. You can just do all this and let the results over the next few days demonstrate the value of this design solution, you can read on a bit further and gain a deeper understanding of how and why this design solution works (the numbered notes below correspond to the numbered steps above), or you can continue your current default habits and see if the problems related to busyness, stress, and overloading go away on their own.

Notes on Each Step of the Turnaround Process

1   Good problem-solving solutions usually possess the following four characteristics: (1) they generate quick and significant progress in terms of solving the problem, (2) they are easy to implement, (3) they take little time to implement, and (4) they cost little to implement. When stressed out, overloaded, over-worked people try this solution, I consistently receive the following feedback: "I get more done in the three 32-minute blocks of time than I used to get done in an entire day!" and "It

feels absolutely marvelous to remain so focused, and accomplish so much, on high-priority items." Index cards are cheap, easy to use, and the process should never take more than about five minutes a day.

2. Likewise, felt tip pens are cheap, easy to use, and get the job done quickly.

3. If you'd like, you can use as many of the 100 cards as you need to dump out everything that's on your mind, in terms of your current and expected future workload, and then select the 10 most important items from the stack. Some people find it comforting to get things off their mind and captured in some sort of written format.

4. Setting a 10-item limit is where the rubber meets the road in terms of reducing stress. Come on; be realistic. Focusing on 10 very important things in your life at any given time is enough. It is very important that you mentally accept this premise. Give it a chance and it won't take you long (probably a day) to totally understand, and literally feel, the value of this strategy. Remember, address the stress first, and then work on solving other problems. This is the beginning of a simple stress-reducing strategy for overloaded people.

5. Quickly write 10 important things on 10 cards. Don't screw around too long with this step. Don't try to get it absolutely right or perfect. Remember, you can

adjust your cards (throw out old ones and add new ones) every day. Of course, you can also alter your plans during the day if you'd like, but in terms of retraining your nervous system (the neuroplasticity stuff) try to stick with a given plan (a stack of 10 index cards) for at least a day.

6 I don't know of any better way to quickly, simply, and accurately prioritize your workload than this flipping-over-index-cards technique.

7 Three is a magical number. It is easy to wrap your mind around the fact that you can make some progress or get closure on at least three important things in a day.

8 All big, intimidating, expensive, complex, time-consuming projects are usually just an aggregation of small, simple, short-duration, inexpensive projects (that can be broken into 32-minute work sessions). You may have already noticed that three 32-minute time blocks add up to a total of 96 minutes. And 96 minutes just happens to be 20 percent of an eight-hour workday. And the 80/20 principle suggests that we get 80 percent of our results from 20 percent of our efforts. Wouldn't it be nice to consistently accomplish 80 percent of your results in one hour and 36 minutes each day and have the rest of the day for bonus activities or unexpected issues that inevitably seem to pop up ... every single working day of your life!

Can you spare little 32-minute blocks of time? Sure you can. I call it the birthday cake phenomena. It is not uncommon to hear busy people express frustration regarding the fact that they can't get everything done. "No way, I can't do that ... I'm swamped!" they say. Want to see if they really have any flexibility in their schedule? Buy a birthday cake, take it to the break room, and tell everyone it's a coworker's birthday. See how many of the "no way, can't do that, I'm swamped" folks show up, stick around, and eat cake. You can do this!

9 I prefer the idea of starting no later than 10 a.m., 2 p.m., and 4 p.m. because it provides a tremendous amount of flexibility. It is not always easy to jump right into your highest priority at the beginning of every day. Actually, considering human nature, it's not terribly realistic to think that you are likely to do that on a consistent basis. However, I find it quite palatable to think in terms of "I only need to stay focused for 32 minutes at a time" and "I'm not forced into a rigid schedule or routine." I just have to get started before a certain time.

10 Repetition is the key to success in forming new habits. I don't think this process will be very difficult for you to repeat because you will realize immediate benefits in terms of how you feel and what you accomplish if you give it a try. Your stress will go down, the thinking part of your brain will be in control of your behavior for more of your workday, and results will likely skyrocket!

It's simply a matter of going full-out each day, creating stress and anxiety and hoping for the best, or slowing down, pausing, resetting each day, and beginning the turnaround process.

That's it for Step 1! Let's move on to Step 2.

| 2

Establishing and Maintaining an Always Follow-Up Reputation

A Design Solution for Improving Follow Up

Years ago, a very smart man named Maynard Rolston taught me that everyone in every organization has one of three follow-up reputations: always, sometimes, or never. My goal is to help you develop and maintain an always follow-up reputation.

Once again, we'll use a design solution to get the job done. However, I want to warn you, this design solution is built around an extremely low-tech resource – a set of files hanging in your desk drawer. I have, pardon the expression, hung in there with my trusty hanging files throughout the onslaught of high-tech alternatives for one huge reason. If you want to develop and maintain an always follow-up reputation, they work better than any alternatives.

I promise I am not a Luddite. I love technological gadgets and use many of them. As a matter of fact, the next chapter includes a design solution totally based on the use of technology. But for now, in terms of establishing and maintaining an always follow-up reputation, I believe a simple and easy-to-maintain hanging file system is best. Give this simple solution a chance. At a minimum, I suggest you use it long enough to retrain your nervous system (30 to 60 days) before switching to any technology-based alternative.

For the record, because of my chosen profession, many software developers ask me to consider endorsing their software solutions for keeping up with work activities. Some of these products are specifically developed by the designer to go along with my teachings. I've tried a lot of these solutions and some of them work pretty well. But so far, not one of them has been as easy to use, or as failsafe, as my drawer of hanging files. The alternative I hear about most often involves setting up some form of electronic files (usually in an e-mail system) and dragging things into these files rather than using paper-based files. This sounds good in theory, but I find it requires much more maintenance and is more difficult to use compared to a hanging file solution. If and when someone comes up with a technology solution that is truly superior, considering my overall objectives for such a system, I'll switch to it.

Here's the bottom line ... in the end, it's all about habits and not the gadgets you use to form the habits. Focus on the habits (getting a more productive group of brain cells firing, and weakening or eliminating the firing of an old unproductive group of brain cells) and use whatever tool gets the job done in the shortest period of time for you.

Good News and Bad News on Follow-Up Reputations

Unfortunately, people are pulled in so many directions these days by self-imposed demands on their time and energy, by the demands of others, and by technological innovations with the ability to summon and demand their attention that it is almost impossible to maintain an always follow-up reputation. That's the bad news. Most of us have grown to expect a certain level of missed deadlines, cancelled appointments, and general lack of follow through.

There are a few people in my circle of business friends, affiliates, and personal friends who are extremely predictable. You can almost always count on them to cancel the first appointment they set with you. Usually it's because of their ongoing habit of over-packing their schedules. After the second or third cancellation, they usually start feeling a bit guilty and show up.

By contrast, we are often surprised when we encounter people who are always on time for appointments, always meet deadlines, always do what they say they will do, and never seem to be in a hurry or under stress.

They always have plenty of high-quality time for you when you need it. When you are with them, they give you their full attention. Here's the good news. Being grounded, centered, reasonably organized and reliable – making others feel that they can really count on you if and when needed – is now a positive differentiator. You are now unique if you do what you say you will do and show up when you say you will show up, in other words ... if you have an always follow-up reputation.

You can't just declare that you have such a reputation and suddenly have it. You can't decide you want such a reputation and buy it. You must earn it over time. Let's talk about a design solution to help you do just that.

The Kitchen Model

Unless you are a complete slob, you are probably already doing most of what I am going to suggest you try in one particular area of your life – your kitchen at home. We are going to talk about how kitchens are usually set up, make some observations, extract some lessons, and then transfer these lessons to your office environment.

Kitchens are often the most organized area of a home. Think about it. You pre-designate places to put things until you need them. This facilitates the creation of excellent storage and retrieval habits. You know exactly where to store things; you know exactly where to find them when you need them.

Let's stop here and reinforce a very important point. Being organized, as it relates to your work life, is more about knowing where to put things, and finding things when you need them, than about neatness. Here's the question you should always be asking when you decide to store something: How will I find this later if and when I need or want it? If you have a good system for storing and retrieving things, neatness will often be a byproduct, but neatness is not the main goal.

Let's explore a few things that go on in a typical kitchen. Most kitchen storage is planned around the dishwasher or sink (wherever you deal with dirty dishes). This is the ultimate gathering place of things you use in the kitchen. When things get dirty, they all pass through this area before being stored ... hopefully.

So, you usually select a drawer near the dishwasher to store frequently used knives, forks, and spoons. The cabinet above the dishwasher is often used for everyday glasses. The everyday plates are stored in the next most convenient cabinet (convenience in this case is defined in terms of proximity to the dishwasher). Items that are used less frequently are stored a bit farther away from the dishwasher. Items that are rarely used (those special holiday plates and items) are stored in the more remote cabinets or the cabinets that are higher up and harder to reach. It all makes perfect sense and makes it extremely easy to form good storage and retrieval habits.

Think about the forks, glasses, and plates you use most often. When you take them out of the dishwasher, you don't even think about what to do with them! Your behavior is automatic. Without using any significant brainpower or energy, you store them away. When you need a fork, glass, or plate you don't even think about how to find it! Your behavior is automatic. Without using any significant brainpower or energy, you reach in the appropriate drawer or cabinet and retrieve them. For example, I don't consciously think about where to put a clean fork. My nervous system is trained to reach into the dishwasher, pick up the fork, instinctively turn to my left, open the silverware drawer, drop the fork in the fork section of the divider inside the drawer, and go on about my business. Because of the way the kitchen is set up in the first place, the system and the process takes care of keeping things in order. Once I form the proper habits, my personal efforts are a minor part of the whole thing.

Now let's transfer this knowledge to your workspace:

- A dishwasher is to your kitchen as your desk chair is to your office (both are the central points for making pre-designated storage decisions).

- A fork, everyday glass, or everyday dish is to your kitchen as an incoming item (for example, a piece of paper) is to your office.

- A drawer or cabinet is to your kitchen as a drawer with hanging files is to your office.

- The process of storage and retrieval is the same in your kitchen and your office.

- Forming good storage and retrieval habits are the same in your kitchen and your office.

- You are you in both places. You automatically store and retrieve things in your kitchen without using any significant brainpower or energy and you can automatically store and retrieve things in your office in the same way.

The Hanging File Design Solution

Here's a step-by-step plan for creating a design solution in your office that will result in an always follow-up reputation.

1 Buy two boxes (25 files per box) of high-quality hanging files. You are going to use these files every working day, so splurge and get high-quality, sturdy files. Color does not matter. Perhaps you want to pick a color you consider fun, interesting, or appealing. That's up to you. Legal or letter does not matter. Most file drawers are adaptable to both. I personally prefer legal simply because they have more room and are slightly easier to get in and out of on an ongoing basis.

2 Pick a drawer that has the capacity to hold 50 hanging files easily. The key to success in selecting this

drawer is location, location, location. In terms of the proximity to your desk chair, the drawer should be no more than a swivel away ... not a swivel and a roll. This drawer will not be used for any sort of permanent storage. It is strictly for storing reminders to prompt you to follow up on important issues and commitments. If your desk does not have such a drawer, you can purchase a file drawer on rollers from most office supply stores. Remove everything from the drawer and do whatever it takes to prepare it to hold 50 hanging files. Make sure the drawer is big enough to hold the 50 files, with plenty of room to spare. It should always be easy to get in and out of a particular file. These files should never end up stuffed full of documents (mostly just single-page reminders or index cards; the pros and cons of each are discussed at the end of this chapter). If there is enough room to get in and out of them easily when they are empty, they should be fine when you put your daily reminder in the files.

3. Label the files in the following manner and put them in the drawer in the following order:

   – Create a file labeled "Follow-Up Forms" or "Forms" (1 file).

   – Create files labeled "1" to "31" (31 separate files).

   – Create files labeled "January" to "December" (12 separate files).

- Create a file labeled with the name of the most important person in your work life, for example, "Robin" (1 file).

- Create a file labeled "Waiting for Response" (1 file).

- Create a file labeled "Meetings" (1 file).

- Create a file labeled "Casual Reading" (1 file).

- Create a file labeled "Purchases" (1 file).

- Create a file labeled "Beyond 1 Year" (1 file).

Okay, that should be 50 files. Most of them should be self-explanatory, but let's go through them and talk about exactly how to use them.

Follow-Up Forms – Demands on your time and energy will typically come to you in one of five forms: paper, voice mails, electronic messages, verbal requests, and things you think of to do. If you can follow up on an item and resolve it in a minute or two, I suggest that you just do it promptly and ignore using the hanging file system. But what about the items you can't follow up on immediately? That's why you set up the hanging files. We want to get these items off your desk and at least temporarily off your mind, and into a place where you will easily encounter them when it's time to follow up. Sometimes, the incoming item will already be in paper form (a memo, an e-mail that can easily be printed, etc.).

If so, simply drop the item in the most appropriate hanging file. For example, if today is the fourth of the month and you plan to follow up on the item the next day, drop it in the hanging file labeled "5." However, some demands on your time and energy come to you in intangible form (verbal requests, your thoughts, a voice mail you need to follow up on, etc.). Use a pre-designed follow-up form for these items. You can design your own form by using a word processing program, the back of recycled sheets of paper ... it doesn't really matter as long as the follow-up form works for you. This is the purpose of the first hanging file. Keep about 10 to 25 blank follow-up forms in this file so you can easily reach for one when you need to create a simple reminder.

At this point, I feel certain I have generated some thoughts about paper and the paperless society. Bear with me and allow me to explain the use of all the files and I will comment on these issues later.

1 to 31 Files – These files will serve as the kitchen drawer-like storage for your daily reminders. Of course, I suggested that you set up 31 of these files because there are no more than 31 days in any given month. These files will help you develop the habit of putting things away when you are not using them instead of allowing them to clutter your office. As in the kitchen, you are much more likely to put things away if you have a pre-designated place for them. It's important to get in the habit of checking the appropriate daily file at the beginning of each workday.

And you might want to take a quick look at the next day's file before you quit working each day.

Between these files and the 10 index cards covered in Chapter 1, you should do a much better job of staying on top of things. These two items work quite well together. For example, I have an index card to remind me of my book writing priority that says "Book GMD10" (GMD10 is my abbreviation for *Getting More Done: 10 Steps for Outperforming Busy People*). Since I have prepared notes and mind maps outlining the main points of each chapter, the outline for this chapter was in my hanging file labeled "4" (today is the fourth of the month). I spread out my index cards first thing this morning, flipped them over and prioritized them; the "Book GMD10" card ended up on top of the stack. I pulled the outline from hanging file "4," set my timer for 96 minutes (when working on book projects, I work in 96-minute rather than 32-minute blocks of time), glanced at the outline ... and starting writing. Keep things simple and keep things flexible. Don't over-think all of this and turn it into something complicated.

When your nervous system gets used to placing reasonable limits on your daily workload, you can eliminate the index cards if you'd like and do all this with the content of your 1 to 31 files, including prioritizing your daily activities by laying out the contents of a file and using the flipping-over technique. I personally like the index cards and continue to use them. For example, I can easily carry them with me and use them to remind me to think about my priorities when I am driving, waiting for an appointment, and so on. If I think of an idea related to accomplishing the item on the card, I make notes on the back of the card to remind me of the idea when I return to my office. The cards are so simple to deal with and so portable, I like having them around.

January to December Files – Okay, I think you are probably getting the hang of this. These files are pre-designated places for follow-up items that extend beyond the current month. On the last working day of each month, pull the contents of the next month's January to December file and place them in the appropriate 1 to 31 files. For example, if I had previously dropped a reminder related to a June 6 meeting in the June file, I might pull it out of the June file on the last working day in May and drop it in the 1 to 31 file labeled "4," "5," or "6" depending on whether or not I need to spend any time preparing for the meeting.

Most Important Person File – Pick the person you interact with the most at work and set up a file with his or her name on it. Robin is my business partner. It is not unusual for me to randomly think of something I want to tell Robin the next time we see or talk to each other. Rather than interrupting my workflow (and hers), I usually just jot a reminder of my thoughts on an index card and drop it in the "Robin" file. These reminders are right there waiting for me the next time we encounter each other. Of course, you can set up as many of these files as you'd like for the various people you interact with on a regular basis. My suggestion is to limit the use of these files to very important people in your life. You don't want to complicate things too much by creating too many files. You can use the same process and put the reminders in the 1 to 31 files you have already set up for most of the people in your circle of influence.

Waiting for Response File – Say you call someone and leave a message to return your call. Drop a reminder or any documents related to what you want to talk about in this file. This clears both your desk and your mind of the unresolved issue. If you promptly receive a returned call, you know right where to go to get the reminder of what you wanted to talk about. If you don't receive a call back, you'll be reminded to follow up the next time you check this file. You can check this file a few times a day to remind yourself of any unreturned calls. Then you can decide if you want to continue following up or pursue an alternative course of action.

Meetings File – This file works much like the Important Person file. It will help you capture and remember those random thoughts that pop into your mind from time to time. Let's say you are required to attend a meeting every Monday. On a Wednesday, you think of something related to the next meeting. Odds are that if you don't capture the thought, you will forget it before next Monday. Jot a reminder on an index card and drop it in this file. Then check the contents of the file before you attend the next meeting and take the cards with you to the meeting.

Casual Reading File – As you encounter things you need or want to read, separate them into two categories: required reading and casual reading. Put required reading items in the appropriate 1 to 31 files based on when you plan to read them (treat them like any other task or project). Put casual reading items in the Casual Reading file. Casual reading items are things you would like to read if you find the time, but there are no significant consequences of not reading them. I suggest you put a date on casual reading items when you place them in the file and periodically throw away anything over 30 days old. For this particular file, I would actually place the contents in a folder inside the hanging file. This allows you to easily grab the folder when you are on the move and perhaps read some of the items while you are waiting for a meeting or appointment, on a train or airplane, and so on.

Purchases File – Use this file for reminders of things you need to get or buy the next time you are headed out to run errands or make purchases. Index cards work fine for this file. You can just grab them and carry them with you when you leave your office.

Beyond 1 Year File – This is a file for long-term planners. Use it just like the 1 to 31 and January to December files; it's just a longer time frame. I don't personally use this file; however, I thought it made sense to consider for people who prefer to cover all the bases.

That's it for Step 2. It shouldn't take you too long to set all this up and learn to use it.

Index Cards versus Follow-Up Forms

Since I have mentioned two types of follow-up reminders, you might be wondering when it is best to use index cards versus follow-up forms. First, let me clarify what I consider to be a follow-up form. A follow-up form is any full-sized sheet of paper you use as a reminder to follow up on something. You can use a blank sheet of notebook paper, the back of a piece of paper you are planning to recycle, or it can be a form developed to meet your specific needs (for example, some of my attorney clients include a place to record the time spent on the activity to help with subsequent billing). I do not have a definitive answer on when to use a particular type of form, but I have some examples and suggestions that should be helpful:

- If I think there may be several follow-up events related to a specific task or project, I like to use full-sized sheets. For example, I recently updated all of my estate planning documents. This involved updating my will, living will, a trust document, durable power of attorney, and several other items related to estate planning. I knew when I first called my attorney that we would probably have several conversations and perhaps a couple of meetings during the updating process. I began this whole process by taking out a follow-up form, writing the name and phone number of my attorney on the top and calling him. This form floated through my 1 to 31 files as the process of updating everything unfolded. This form became, in effect, the lead or cover sheet for this project. As I write this, there is only one more item to take care of and the project will be complete. Since the item remaining is clearly in my attorney's court, the original follow-up form is now in my Waiting for Response hanging file. This follow-up form has notes on our conversations, several one-liner references to e-mails exchanged (the e-mails are stored in an electronic file on my computer in case I need them), his initial estimate of the cost of his services, appointment times and dates, and anything else I thought I might need to document regarding our interactions. It is extremely rare, but sometimes I add a second follow-up form for projects that cover an extended period of time or a high volume of follow-up activities.

- On the contrary, a lot of these files are mainly for capturing my thoughts (the Meetings File, Important Person File, Purchases File, etc.). I feel very comfortable using index cards for these reminders.

- There have been times when I started out with an index card and then decided I needed more room for notes. In this situation, I often tape or staple the index card to a full-sized sheet and use the full-sized sheet going forward.

- In the end, I don't think it matters which you use. The important thing is developing the habit of creating some form of reminder to place in the appropriate file. I will caution you to be careful if you use both types of forms in the same file. Sometimes you might pull the full-sized sheets out of a hanging file and inadvertently forget to pull out the smaller index cards.

Paper and Paperlessness

As for those of you who are eagerly anticipating the paperless society and for those who view the use of paper in a digital world unusual or objectionable, here are my comments:

- I have run across a few (very few) people who are closing in on the creation of the paperless office. Unfortunately, they still have to interact with others who are not seeking such goals and who continue to bombard them with paper. And if these other people, for example, happen to be important clients and don't care about your paperless preference, sometimes you cannot totally ignore documents that spew out of their paper-based world. So this system offers some value even to paperless society advocates.

- I have run across people with extremely sophisticated systems to eliminate physical documents. These systems usually involve computers, scanners, software, and so on. In the end, most of them are quite labor intensive. Considering the five ways most incoming items enter your life, paper seems to be the easiest way to keep up with everything. As I mentioned, some item are already in paper form and others (such as your thoughts or verbal requests) can easily be converted to a paper reminder.

- Use your imagination and be innovative when creating reminders for your follow-up files. For example, if someone sends me a long e-mail, memo, or electronic document, and I need to follow up on it later, I only print out the first page of the document to use as my reminder. Then I create an electronic folder (if I don't already have one set up for that category of items) and drag the whole file into the archive folder. On the day I have decided to follow up, I pull the reminder from my 1 to 31 files and then turn to my computer and pull up the entire document. Likewise, if I plan to work on a large, say 40 to 50 page hardcopy document, I copy the first page of the document to use as a reminder for my 1 to 31 files and put the large document in my reference files (the topic of the next chapter) until I need it.

If none of the previous comments work for you, use whatever technology resources you'd like to accomplish the same thing. I'm an experimenter, so I have tried a lot of different ways to do things. I agree that most everything I have talked about can be done with technology. I just think the hanging file system is the easiest to set up and use. People are more likely to stick with things that are easy. And with this particular setup, I have no problems with power outages, computer crashes, viruses, and the like.

The bottom line on this idea ... implement some kind of system to develop and maintain an always follow-up reputation. It will make you unique!

3

Finding Things Quickly When You Need Them

How Frustrating Is That!?!

How many times does it have to happen before you do something about it? Something triggers a thought about an article you read about six months ago. Now you want to find it again. You remember you saved it because you thought it might be helpful in the future and, sure enough, you were right! Based on what you remember, it seems right on point with an issue you want to discuss with your boss. You know it's somewhere in your office. Off and on over the last few days, you've probably spent over an hour looking for the article. Finally, you give up ... forget it!

A month later, after the window of opportunity to talk with your boss has passed, you find the article when you're looking for something else in a stack of papers under another stack of papers on the back corner of your credenza. The article is on the bottom of the stack. Unfortunately, you still haven't found what you were actually looking for at the time.

Let's talk about things you might consider doing with such an article the first time you encounter it. Let's talk about how to store things in a manner that easily allows you to find them when you need them.

**You Don't Understand …
I Know Where Everything Is in This Mess**

First, let's deal with a thought that might have come up when you read the last few paragraphs: "I know my office looks like a disaster. But trust me; it's my mess and I know where everything is in here."

Ha, ha … that's a good one! I might even buy into this myth if I didn't know better. In addition to classroom instruction and writing books on this topic, I have a lot of experience helping people physically implement my ideas in their workspace. Here's what usually happens. When I first visit their office to help them get things in order, many clients defiantly make the above statement or a statement similar to it. They don't apologize for their mess, and I certainly don't expect an apology, but often their statements clearly fall into the category of "thou doth protest too much." So we get busy and start going through the piles and getting everything organized. Inevitably, at some point in the session they pick up a piece of paper and say, "Damn, I've been looking for this for six months!" Oops, they forgot what they told me earlier.

I've learned that when clients make their bold statement in the beginning of our time together to let it go and just wait for the "oops" moment to reinforce any potential lessons related to the "I know where everything is in this mess" mentality. Let's come up with a better way to store and find things.

Back to the Kitchen

Once again, the kitchen model works well. We need to pre-designate places to put important things so we know where to put them when we want to store them and know how to find them easily when we need them. However, in the case of reference files, the storage is more permanent. Follow-up items, the items we discussed in the previous chapter, come and go as you work on and complete them. They move in and out of the 50 follow-up files. However, reference files are the end of the line for many documents. You simply want to keep them for some reason, usually because you think you might want or need to refer (hence the name reference file) to them in the future.

Examples of Reference Files

This isn't a new concept – everyone has reference files. They include things like client files, project files, articles, old memos, correspondence, instruction manuals, binders, photos, meeting notes, and so on. You get the idea.

If it's something you want to keep, and it does not belong in your follow-up files because there is no current follow-up activity related to it, it's a reference file.

Get Ready for Counter-Intuitive Thinking

We're going to create a system that makes it incredibly easy to put things away when you want to keep them (versus having them stacked on your desk or stuffed somewhere until you get around to doing something with them) and makes it incredibly easy to find them when you need them. But there's a catch! You need to let go of alphabetical filing. Having file cabinets full of alphabetically labeled files made sense in the past. But now, with the help of Google and other search engines, we've learned to comfortably look for things electronically with search commands. So, we're only going to label our files with numbers! No letters, no words … nothing but numbers on the hanging-file tabs. I predict once you get used to it, it will make perfect sense to you.

Setting Up Reference Files

Setting up reference files takes some time on the front end. As a matter of fact, this is probably the most time-consuming task in this book. You might need to block out a half-day to set up the reference files explained in this chapter. However, your ROE (return on effort) will be swift and significant. After the initial set up, it requires some effort to maintain, but not too much. I'll explain how to take care of that easily. And odds are once you get these files set up, you will be happy you took the time to do so for the rest of your working career. Having a good reference filing system is a true game-changer in terms of your productivity and professionalism.

For illustration purposes, let's assume you keep your reference files in a standard four-drawer, black, upright file cabinet.

1   Preferably, your four-drawer filing cabinet is a sturdy, reasonable quality cabinet with drawers about 26 inches deep in the direction the files face. Drawers of this size comfortably hold about 80 hanging files. Therefore, you can create 320 (80 x 4) reference file locations. Letter or legal size does not matter. I personally prefer legal. This allows me to put most any document in a file without folding it.

2   To set up your new reference filing system, create four sets of 80 files labeled "1" to "80" (use the plastic tabs that come with the files to create the labels). The numeric reference is all you need to put on the label. To make this step easy, I use a standard Avery form – form number 5267 – which is actually designed to create 80 return address labels. The template for the form can be found under the "Tools" menu on most word processing programs (typically

you can find the Avery template options under the "Letters and Mailing," then the "Envelopes and Labels" choice on the drop down). Of course, you can use other methods, including handwriting the labels, for this step.

3. Place the 80 labels on or inside the plastic tabs. If you use the Avery labels, just stick them on the front facing side of the plastic tab. If you use other methods, slide them inside the tab.

4. Now place the tabs in the slots on the hanging files. When displayed properly, the facing side of the tab should be slanting toward the back of the hanging file (or file cabinet drawer). If you are using legal files, you should be able to stagger the labels six across from left to right (five across if you are using letter size hanging files.) After completing a row of six (or five) tabs, shift back to the left side of the next file and create a second row. Keep this up until you have four sets of 80 files numbered "1" to "80." Suggestion: Place the tabs on the front edge of the hanging file. This is a minor issue, but prevents you from obscuring the label if the file contains a lot of documents.

5. Drop 80 labeled files in each of the four file cabinet drawers in numerical order (files 1 to 80 in each drawer). You now have 320 storage places for things you might want to find later. Remember, you're much more likely to put things away if you know where to

put them. Having these pre-designated storage spaces is half the battle of having a good reference filing system.

Now let's set up the "find them when you need them" design solution.

1   Create an electronic spreadsheet with the following three columns (portrait or landscape orientation does not matter, I prefer landscape so I will have more room for keywords if I need it):

File #. This column only has to be large enough to hold a location code. For example, if you decide to store a document in the first hanging file in the top drawer of your four-drawer filing cabinet, you might use the code BF1-1 as code for this location (B = black, F = file, 1 = top drawer, 1 = file No. 1). If you store something in the eighth hanging file in the bottom drawer of the cabinet, you might use the code BF4-8 (assuming you decide to number the drawers one to four, from top to bottom). Of course, you can make up any code that makes sense to you.

File Name. This column only has to be large enough to hold the words that you might put on a file tab if you were planning to file alphabetically, for example "Doe, John" or "XYZ project."

Keywords. Use the rest of the column width for this section.

2   Look over this example before proceeding. Let's assume the first reference file you want to set up is to store documents related to your computer. And the second file you want to set up is to store documents related to your employee benefits. Here's how the first two rows of your spreadsheet might look:

File #	File Name	Keywords
BF1-1	Computer	Apple, iMac, One-to-One, Apple Care
BF1-2	Benefits	401K, Health, Dental, Disability, Insurance

3   Continue this coding, recording, and filing process until you have information on all your reference file items listed on your spreadsheet and in the appropriate drawer and hanging file.

4   Save the spreadsheet and back it up as often as you feel necessary. When you want to locate a reference file item in the future, go to the spreadsheet "Find" command, enter the file name or any keyword in the search field, and press enter. In less than a second, you should know exactly where to find the item you need.

Tips

- Print a hard copy of the spreadsheet periodically as an additional backup. Store the hardcopy in a place that is easy to find. I keep my hardcopy backup in my "Follow-Up Forms" hanging file (described in the previous chapter).

- Create all the files you might use in the near future at one time. In other words, keep empty, pre-numbered files as pre-designated places to store things. You are much more likely to maintain the system if you don't have to stop and set up a hanging file every time you want to store a new reference item.

- After you set up your initial batch of files, always use the "Find" command to see if you already have a file that will work for any new items. For example, if I decide to store a memo from my client John Doe, and know (or think) I have an existing file for this client, I would search for "Doe" and check it out. If I did have an existing file, there would be no need to set up another one. I would just drop the item in the existing file.

- Use a pre-designated box, file, or tray as a storage location to accumulate reference file items temporarily. You do not need to stop and file these items too often; once a week is probably fine. I prefer to store reference file items temporarily in an inbox I keep on a shelf in my office and process them all at once on Friday afternoons.

- Purge your reference files periodically. I go through mine every December and toss things I no longer think I might need. When I discard an item, I also delete the entries on the spreadsheet for that item and put the word "Open" in the File Name field. When filing future items, you can easily enter the word "Open" in the "Find" command search field and it will take you to the next available empty row on the spreadsheet.

- If you are creative, you can use this same process to store and easily find anything. For example, I keep exactly 1,000 books in my office. I consider them reference items because I often refer to them when preparing to teach or write. Using a process similar to the one just described (with slight alterations), I label all my books and list them on a spreadsheet. In the case of the books, I just put a small label on the spine with a number on it (1 to 1,000). That number, in turn, goes in the first column of my spreadsheet. I put the title of the book in the second column, and the author and any keywords in the third column. Once again, I can use the "Find" command to locate any book in seconds. There is no magic to the number 1,000. I just decided 1,000 books is enough based on the bookshelf capacity of my office. When I get a new book that I want to keep, an old book that I no longer use has to go. Since the computer can find any book in seconds, it doesn't matter that they are not grouped by category. You can use a similar process to keep up with binders, office supplies (put them in plastic containers and label them with a locator code), or anything that can be stored on a shelf, in a drawer, in a cabinet, etc.

- Keep this simple. There are numerous software and Web-based solutions available to help you maintain reference files if you decide you want to implement a more sophisticated system. You can also find consultants to help you set up a system that meets your needs. But I prefer starting with the simplest solution. I keep up with a huge number of reference files and have tried many of the commercially available products. A simple spreadsheet still works best for me.

This is a Huge Step!

All this may sound like a mundane project and it will take a little effort on the front end to get it done. However, this is a big deal in terms of productivity. You probably won't realize how big a deal it is until about a week after you've set all this up and start using it. Putting aside all the time you will save over the long haul, this is going to make you feel good several times a day. You are going to be very happy you did this every time it's time to find something!

Pause

Okay, let's pause a moment and summarize. If you have done everything so far, you should already feel quite different (in a very positive way). You know how to easily capture, prioritize, and focus on the 10 most important things in your work life every day, you know how to efficiently and effectively stay on top of incoming items in order to maintain an always follow-up reputation, and you know how to store and easily find items. You've made a lot of progress in a short period of time! Seven steps to go and you will be a role model for a grounded, centered, highly productive, happy person.

4

Absolutely Ruthless E-mail Management

The Main Problem with E-mail

E-mail is one of those technology solutions that sometimes creates more problems than it solves. It can be a wonderful tool for communicating with people ... or it can be an energy-draining, productivity-killing nightmare.

In order to get e-mail problems under control quickly, we need to understand the main reason e-mail has become such a big stress-inducing issue. Let's step away from e-mail for a minute and just focus on stress. What causes stress? Stress and anxiety are typically the results of some type of fear. So the question is: With regard to e-mails, what do people fear? My best guess is that people most fear missing something important.

A story in the *New York Times* titled "Hooked on Gadgets, and Paying a Mental Price" relays the experience of a start-up entrepreneur who missed an important e-mail from a suitor who wanted to buy his company. According to the article, "the message had slipped by him amid an electronic flood." He finally noticed the message 12 days later while sifting through old e-mails. Luckily he salvaged the deal; however, I suspect this experience increased his fear, and probably the fears of anyone who read the article, of missing something important because of the ongoing e-mail tsunami.

Everyone understands that e-mails enter our lives with little or no effort on our part. Unfortunately, it takes some effort on our part to make them quickly exit our lives. Otherwise, just like paper, e-mails piles up in a hurry. If 100 e-mails come into your life each day and you discard half, you're still going to have 18,250 e-mails stacked up at the end of the year. It's easy to miss something important in a stack that size!

Once again, we need a design solution to deal with this situation.

The Root of All E-mail Evil

I'm going to make a bold statement:

> Most problems related to e-mail center around one issue: how long you typically allow an e-mail to sit in your inbox.

Keep your e-mail inbox in order and the stress related to e-mail will take care of itself. Specifically, clear your inbox at least once a day and most of your e-mail problems will be solved.

Many of you are now shaking your head thinking, "I can't do that! No way. You've got to be kidding. That's impossible!" But, I've seen it work with too many people. Assuming your primary responsibility is not processing e-mail all day – in other words, e-mail is just a tool you use to communicate with clients and coworkers – emptying your inbox once a day will greatly reduce your stress and anxiety.

Stress related to e-mail is primarily related to the number of messages in your inbox waiting for your attention. Having five legitimate unread and unanswered e-mails is not typically stressful. Having 50, 500, 5,000, or more is a problem.

Think about it. What if you never emptied your regular mailbox? You just left everything in there and let the postal carrier continue to cram things in day after day. You left bills there until it was time to pay them, magazines there until you found the time to read them, cards and letters from friends there in case you wanted to pull them out and look at them again later. Of course in a short time, in addition to having a disgruntled postal carrier, you would never be able to find anything. And the stress related to what's in your mailbox and what you might be missing in all that junk would continue to increase. Think of your inbox in the same way. It's just an electronic space instead of a box!

So the big question, since many of you may have thousands of e-mails waiting for your attention, is how do you empty your inbox?

Here We Go!

1. Get ruthless! Do whatever it takes to get into a ruthless, e-mail annihilating frame of mind. Most of you are familiar with the game Whac-a-Mole. Little critters pop up out of holes ... and you whack them with a mallet! That's all there is to it! It's a relatively mindless game – but quite fun. Well, get ready to play a similar game I call Whac-a-Mail. There actually is great value in developing a game-mentality in dealing with e-mail. You win if, at the end of the day, your e-mail inbox is empty. Empty is better than three; three is better than 10; 10 is definitely better than 50. Keep score. Even after you get rid of the current backlog, get into this frame of mind once a day and annihilate the little e-mail critters.

2. Block out some uninterrupted time for your first game of Whac-a-Mail. If at all possible, make the initial marathon clearing of your inbox a one-shot project. Based on experience with clients, you are going to feel absolutely great when you complete this step. Process your current backlog in a series of 32-minute blocks of time with short five-minute breaks

between sessions. If you have a typical mix of important, maybe important, unimportant, who knows, and junk e-mail in your inbox, budget one 32-minute block of time for every 300 e-mails in your inbox. So, if you have 2,000 old e-mails sitting in your inbox, budget about a half-day to process them. I'm not talking about answering them. The goal right now is to get them out of your inbox. Hopefully, you will get the job done much quicker than this. The first time is the worst time with this process. Once your inbox is empty, the ongoing daily maintenance is relatively simple.

3   Sort your inbox. Sort the e-mails in your inbox in a way that makes it easiest for you to evaluate them. Some people suggest sorting them in "Date Received" order. In working with clients, I find that sorting them in "From" order works pretty well. This allows you to eliminate huge blocks of e-mails at a time. For example, you may have large blocks of e-mails stored in your inbox from people who no longer work for your organization or for whatever reason are no longer a part of your life. You can quickly whack them out of your e-mail life. Think about it and sort them in whatever way works best for you. Or sort them multiple ways during the process. Just get rid of them!

4   Perform e-mail triage. Think of yourself as an e-mail emergency-room physician. Set up three electronic folders in your e-mail system labeled "Later

Maybe," "Code Blue," and "Keepers." It's critical that you do not stop during your game of Whac-a-Mail to process any of the e-mails! At this point, clearing your inbox is your highest priority. Start attacking the backlog and make the following decisions as quickly as possible:

Dead E-mails – Certain opportunities (related to the subject of the particular e-mail) are already dead or near dead. There is no chance your attention will revive them. Perhaps you feel the information contained in the e-mail is, as television mobster Tony Soprano often said, "dead to me" – you no longer want or need it.

Delete the e-mail or, if possible, select and delete an entire block of e-mails. Remember ... be ruthless. There is a momentum to the process of throwing things away, or in the case of e-mails, deleting things. The first few items are usually the hardest to deal with. After a certain number of items, you usually get into a "this feels good, let's pick up the pace" mood. Stop over-thinking things and morph into an e-mail discarding demon!

Later Maybe E-mails – Opportunities related to some e-mails will survive whether you pay immediate attention to the e-mail or not. Discard these e-mails if at all possible. If you just can't get comfortable deleting them, drag them into the "Later Maybe" file.

Code Blue E-mails – Hospitals worldwide use emergency codes to alert staff members to various emergency situations. Code Blue is generally used to indicate a patient requiring immediate resuscitation.

Make it extremely rare, but if you really think certain opportunities will only survive if you address them in the very near-term future (but not until after you finish your initial game of Whac-a-Mail), drag these into the Code Blue file.

Keepers – You may have e-mails that don't necessarily fit into any of the three triage categories. No action is required on your part; you just want to keep them. Drag these into the Keepers file.

5   Continue triage until your inbox is empty! This will not be near as difficult to do as you might think. I am usually all about slowing down and establishing a reasonable, steady pace. Not in this case, develop a "need for speed" and kick e-mail butt!

Ongoing Ideas for Managing Your Inbox

Here are some additional tips to keep your e-mail inbox in order:

- Quickly convert any Code Blue e-mails into index card reminders and process them using the ideas covered in Chapters 1 and 2.

- Keep your Later Maybe file to a minimum. Look for ways to eventually delete e-mails in this file if at all possible. In any case, they are stored there if you need them, so don't spend any time stressing over them.

- Do what you can with your e-mail filters. Although technology will never provide the total solution, filters can be helpful.

- Play Whac-a-Mail once a day. After the first day, it should take very little time to finish a game.

- As appropriate, set up other archive files to go along with the three you have already set up. For example, I have files set up for "Netflix," "Purchases," and "Resources." I use these to keep up with e-mails related to the back and forth movement of Netflix videos, e-mails related to online purchase confirmations, and links to interesting Web sites, articles, videos, and so on, that friends send me. I also occasionally set up temporary archive files. For example, if I know I'm going to being sending and receiving a lot of e-mails related to a project – and I might want to refer to these from time to time – I'll set up a temporary file for the duration of the project. This allows me to keep things I might need, keep the clutter out of my inbox, and quickly get rid of them when the project is complete.

- Stop using your e-mail inbox as a "To Do" list. It was not designed for this purpose. Use the index cards discussed in Chapter 1.

- Do not use your e-mail inbox for filing things. It was not designed for this purpose. Use the hanging file systems discussed in Chapters 2 and 3.

- Use your e-mail inbox to receive and ever-so-briefly store e-mails. This is its purpose!

| 5

Managing Meeting Mania

Stop the Meeting Mania!

Mania is defined as "having an excessive and intense interest in or enthusiasm for something." This book is all about addressing big picture issues that might be responsible for workplace productivity problems. If I were rounding up the usual productivity-killing suspects, excessive and inefficient meetings would be high on the list. Although no one likes to admit it, many people, especially in large organizations, seem to have an excessive and intense interest in or enthusiasm for meetings. When I ask clients about the meeting culture of their organization, the most common response is eye-rolling. I am not against meetings, but I am for minimizing or eliminating them if you are genuinely too busy to attend a lot of meetings in the 24 hours available each day.

Hold your thoughts on meetings a moment.

Here's the bottom line on working through any time-shortage problem:

- *Accept the fact that time is not variable.* Start with this premise in developing any strategy to deal with a time-shortage problem. Mentally eliminate the possibility of a 25-hour, 26-hour, 27-hour, or longer day if you plan to continue residing and working on this particular planet.

- *Place your total focus on the other side of the equation.* Accept the fact that any solution to a time-shortage problem must involve an overall reduction in planned activities.

You now have two excellent sub-options:

- Eliminate low-value or no-value activities (the effectiveness or "doing the right things" approach).

- Reduce the amount of time it takes to complete high-value and unavoidable activities (the efficiency or "doing things right" approach).

Now, just apply this kind of thinking to meetings.

Beware of Busyness

In 2002, the *Harvard Business Review* published a fascinating article titled "Beware the Busy Manager" by

Heike Bruch and Sumantra Ghoshal. The article discussed the result of a comprehensive study of very busy people. The subjects of the study were smart people working for large, sophisticated, highly credible organizations. These people had significant responsibilities and were very busy. Unfortunately, the study revealed that roughly 90 percent of the things these busy people were doing with their time every day did not matter. In other words, most of their activities were not important in terms of advancing the strategic objectives of their organizations.

Remember, when you are busy, you are putting yourself in the worst possible state of mind for making good decisions about what is important and what is not. The functional areas of your brain that help you plan, organize, make good decisions, and control impulsive behavior are likely shut down or severely inhibited. You are not a bad person; you are just temporarily operating in a highly diminished brainpower mode. Don't let busyness diminish your ability to make good decisions about the amount of time you choose to spend in meetings.

The Mathematics of Available Meeting Time and the Plan

Let's talk about a step-by-step plan for dealing with meetings. Holding time constant at 24 hours a day, let's talk about things on the other side of the equation.

1   Start with a little math based on your personal body rhythms. I'll use my best guess to illustrate this idea

and you can adjust your numbers as you deem appropriate. Don't try to get this perfect, just go with your best guess:

– Sleep – 8 hours

– Eating and preparing or acquiring meals – 3 hours

– Personal hygiene – 1 hour

– Work activities – 8 hours

– Everything else – 4 hours (rest, relaxation, fun, energy restoration activities, commuting, child care, paying bills, home maintenance, etc.)

Right off the bat things don't look so good do they? Well, one of the reasons is that some anthropologists and other scientists who study such things think we are probably designed to work about four hours a day. That is, back in the old days, primitive people spent about four hours a day looking for food and the rest of the day singing, dancing, sleeping, having sex, and basically partying. On second thought, maybe they weren't so primitive. Anyhow, looking for food back then was most people's profession. Before refrigerators were invented allowing humans to store food, people had to go out every day in search of the next meal. But as they say, at this point in history, the eight-hour workday is what it is. Considering the anatomical body design that our partying ancestors handed down to us, it's definitely not a good idea to try and extend the modern workday beyond eight hours. Play around with the above math until you are satisfied that, at least on paper, you have designed a relatively balanced day for yourself.

2   Next, consistently try to get enough sleep as often as possible. Sleep appears to be much more important than most people think. Scientists previously thought that the purpose of sleep was to let your body rest and restore itself. They now know this is pretty much true with one huge exception – the brain. The human brain is incredibly active during your sleeping hours. It is working on some very important things ... things that are critically important if you desire to have a productive day the next day.

For example, in terms of your mental health and stability, your brain processes the events of your day during sleep. It sorts through the events and tries to make sense of everything. That's why things that seem like such a big deal in the evening are often relatively insignificant the next morning. Your brain considers the event and often says, "Whatever!" and then discards the memory of the event, or puts everything in some sort of reasonable perspective. Memory consolidation (reinforcing new things you learned during the day) also occurs during sleep. Basically, a lot of extremely important things take place while you are sleeping to prepare you for the next day.

It's simple, eliminate sleep and you eliminate all of these highly important activities. Based on what I have read, I'd be very careful about cutting sleep back to less than six hours in a 24-hour period. So, get at least six, seven, eight, or nine hours sleep most nights. If this is just impossible (for example, working mothers or fathers with newborns), research indicates that naps are very good for you!

3. Okay, holding time for sleep as constant as possible, jockey around with the other numbers and make sure the math works.

Now, let's get to this issue of meetings. Obviously, we always want the amount of time allocated to meetings to be a subset of the eight hours allocated to work. Let's try to be realistic and do the math on that eight-hour block of time (eight hours equals 480 minutes). Remember the index cards you created in Chapter 1? Here are some minimums:

- 32 uninterrupted minutes – priority No. 1 for the day

- 32 uninterrupted minutes – priority No. 2 for the day

- 32 uninterrupted minutes – priority No. 3 for the day

- 32 minutes – making some progress on priorities No. 4 through 10

- 32 minutes – checking e-mails, voicemails, etc.

- 32 minutes – ramp down and ramp up time between tasks

- 32 minutes – totally unexpected events

- 96 minutes – an incredibly generous allowance for meetings (3 x 32 minutes each)

- 160 minutes – everything else

The purpose of playing around with these numbers is to help you think through and figure this out. Don't get hung up on any particular number and throw the baby out with the bathwater (for example, the 32-minute block allocated to totally unexpected events ... I agree that's funny when you consider reality some days). The value that math brings to the table is that math can be very sobering. Sometimes math can show you the folly of your plans and serve as a sobering reality check.

The point is, would you consider the day outlined above a pretty good day, a reasonably balanced day, a satisfying day? I would! I blocked out time to focus on my three most important priorities, time to make some progress on seven other important things, and even allocated some time for unexpected events. And still, I had quite a bit of time for other activities.

Why the 96 minutes allocated to meetings? What's the logic behind that? When in doubt, and in the absence of any other deciding factor, I always default to the 80/20 principle. If we, in fact, get 80 percent of our results from 20 percent of our efforts, I wouldn't allocate more than 20 percent of a workday to meetings. Spending more than 20 percent of your time in meetings every day is rarely a good use of your time.

I understand that I have already asked you to allocate 20 percent of your day to your top three priorities, and attending a meeting can certainly be one of your priorities for the day. However, there is no rule that prevents you from using 80/20 thinking over and over in different areas of your life to improve things – by shifting more and more activities from the unproductive to productive category.

Now we have a budget for meetings. No more than 96 minutes most days. There are always exceptions. That's reality. But remember, an exception is something that is not a general rule or pattern. Unless your job is to literally sit in meetings all day, more than 96 minutes allocated to meeting time should not occur very often.

Here are some other things to consider:

- Plan any necessary meetings to fit within your budget. Make few or no exceptions, at least until you have your workload under control. I suggest no more than three meetings a day and meetings no longer than 32 minutes each (of course, shorter is fine). This 32-minute meeting format is similar to the 9 mph or 19 mph speed limit in apartment complexes. People are more likely to notice and comply with an oddball number. We're trying to solve this busyness problem for you. A budget of three meetings a day is extremely generous. Of course, this in no way implies that you must conduct or attend three meetings every day. Just consider this budget your maximum.

- Make not having a meeting your default position. Most people schedule a meeting or agree to participate in a meeting at the drop of a hat. Until you get your busyness under control, do the opposite. Before scheduling or attending a meeting, consider any and all alternatives (phone call, memo, etc.).

What about those meetings your boss requires you to attend? If you have implemented the ideas in Chapters 1 and 2, you are now in a much better position to perhaps deal with this situation. I'm not promising these ideas can solve problems related to a narcissistic or control-freak boss. But, if your boss keeps piling on the meetings, discuss your top 10 priorities and the contents of your 1 to 31 files. Ask whether or not you should eliminate some of the things you have already planned in order to attend more meetings. Maybe, just maybe, you'll be cut some slack.

- If you have control over whether or not to attend a meeting, determine the need to attend the meeting based on your 10 top priorities. Ask: Will this meeting enhance or inhibit my ability to stay focused and get closure on any of my 10 most important items?

When you have no benchmarks for making decisions about whether or not to attend a meeting, you are likely to automatically accept meeting invitations. When you compare the meeting objectives with your personal objectives and they don't match up, it is probably not necessary for you to attend the meeting. Turn it down!

Although some people frequently and vocally complain about having to attend an excessive number of meetings, these same people would probably be disappointed if they were not included. For some people, being included in meetings has become a status symbol. Here's a better status symbol: Develop the reputation as someone who does not measure your value by the number of meetings you are invited to, or committees you serve on. Have a reputation that prompts people to say and think, "Don't ask that person to attend your meeting unless the meeting objectives are clearly stated, the meeting is well organized, well executed, the leader has the reputation for starting and ending on time, and the objectives are relevant to their priorities." I am not against meetings! Meeting with others is the best way to get things done ... at times. I am against meetings that do not matter!

- If you are the meeting leader, develop and stick with a structured meeting process. Stick with this particular format until you feel your workday and workload are back under control. Then alter the parameters as appropriate when you have achieved your goal of working at a more relaxed pace:

– Be an absolute fanatic about starting on time (preferably not on the hour or half-hour).

– Block out 32 minutes for the meeting. If you are focused, you can accomplish a tremendous amount in 32 minutes.

– State the type of meeting: discussion only, discussion and decision, information/briefing only, information/briefing and decision, etc.

– State the meeting topic in 15 words or less. Ask one person to restate their understanding of the topic. Ask if anyone else needs clarity before continuing.

– At the beginning of the meeting, ask everyone to pause for 60 seconds and jot down any thoughts they might have related to the topic. No talking during the pause. The pausing idea, which might seem a bit strange, comes from some meeting guidelines outlined in *The Innovator's Handbook* by Vincent Nolan. The ideas in Nolan's book are based on observing, filming, and studying thousands of meetings to determine what works and what doesn't work in terms of conducting effective and efficient meetings. You will generate more thoughts and get more meaningful feedback in a meeting if you allow this pause for a moment of reflection.

- Maintain control and formally debrief the meeting participants' ideas and comments. Call on senior people last, meeting dominators last (if at all), encourage but do not force everyone to participate, do not allow personal attacks, do not allow off-topic rambling (make a note of any off-topic comments and promise to address them outside the meeting if they are important). In short, maintain control over the meeting and accomplish the stated objectives.

- Five minutes before the scheduled ending of the meeting, summarize the main aspects of the meeting. Use a timer and make sure everyone can hear when it goes off. Draw conclusions, make decisions, agree on any follow-up items to be completed as a result of the meeting, designate a single individual to take primary responsibility for each follow-up item, set a deadline for each follow-up item, and take care of anything else that needs to be done.

- Adjourn the meeting. Be an absolute fanatic about ending on time.

Overloading is Overloading

Okay, let's be realistic. Maybe you can't accomplish everything using the 32-minute meeting format. But the 32-minute meeting should become the rule and longer meetings should become the rare exceptions.

Think about what we are trying to accomplish with this step. Since we cannot control time, we must learn to use our limited time in the most rational way possible. Our choices are to eliminate activities, or get the things done that need to be done in less time. Until you get things under control, go on a meeting diet and compress the amount of time needed to get the job done.

Synergy ... the Magic Word!

You should now be five days and five ideas into this book. At this point, you should be noticing some synergies. For example, it is easier to make a decision on attending a meeting (outlined in this chapter) if you know your most important priorities (outlined in Chapter 1). Time available should be trending upward, clutter and lost or misplaced items should be trending downward, stress should be down and productivity should be up.

Now let's move on and discuss more details on how to stay on top of key tasks and projects.

| 6

Goldilocks Planning

Just Right!

In one sense, *Goldilocks* is a story about the discovery of what is "just right." Basically, the main character of the story, Goldilocks, is guilty of breaking and entering the home of a threesome of variable-sized bears (large, medium, and small), sampling their food and trying out various pieces of their furniture. Goldilocks seemed to be most interested in rambling about the bears' home trying to find things that were congruent with her body size and personal taste. Setting aside Goldilocks' criminal activities for a moment, we can learn a valuable lesson from her related to planning. Goldilocks was very focused on getting things just right. That's a great goal for planning a project ... getting things just right.

I frequently observe two major mistakes related to planning: over-planning and under-planning. With planning, sometimes people seem to have a hard time getting things just right. That's what this chapter is about ... just right planning.

We're Not Talking about Putting a Man or Woman on the Moon

The goal of this book is to help busy people quickly get things turned around and back under control. So, this chapter is not about planning for comprehensive, long-term, strategic projects. We're talking about a simple planning process for those everyday projects that we all have to get done. This process can certainly work for more complex projects, but it's primarily designed to get quick results and provide quick relief from the stress of mismanaging or putting off important projects.

Back to Einstein's Wisdom and Models

In general, plans exist for people, not the other way around. And plans should be as simple as possible, but no simpler. In the simplest terms, planning can be divided into three phases:

1. What you plan to do
2. How you plan to do it
3. Doing it

That's it! We're going to develop a planning process that addresses these three steps.

Goldilocks Planning | 83

By now you know I like design solutions based on models that already work well in one area of life and can be transferred to your work environment (sometimes with slight alterations). So what can we use as a model for planning? A couple of ideas come to mind.

Nature is always a great teacher and pregnancy is, of course, a natural process. Much can be learned about planning by thinking about pregnancy. There is a definite beginning. And if all is as it should be, the beginning is fun and exciting. That's the way a good plan should start. It should be fun and exciting. Then, in the middle of a pregnancy, things are not necessarily so fun and exciting, but you hang in there and do what you have to do to keep things on track. Likewise, sometimes things begin to drag a bit in the middle of a work project. You'll need to keep this in mind as you develop your project plan, since there is no Mother Nature-like force to keep you focused and make sure you follow up on important things. And again, if all goes as it should, a pregnancy has a well-defined ending, in other words you get closure ... oh yeah, and you also get a baby.

Let's look at one more interesting planning model: MapQuest. For those of you who might not be familiar with it, MapQuest is a Web site to help you with your travel plans. It's simple to learn and easy to use. On the MapQuest home page, there are several things prominently displayed: a section clearly labeled "Start" with blank spaces to enter an address, a section clearly labeled "End" with blank spaces to enter an address, and a large button labeled "Get Directions." When you click the "Get Directions" button, MapQuest does its thing and gives you detailed, step-by-step directions on how to get from where you are to where you want to go. All you have to do is get in your car and execute the step-by-step plan.

Clarity

Pregnancy and MapQuest seem to be unusual things to compare. But what are the common elements of these two models?

The End – What you want to accomplish is clear. In one case, Mother Nature takes care of clarity for you. You are going to have a baby. In the case of MapQuest, you are prompted to clearly state your travel destination. If you put anything vague in the "End" field, the computer keeps prompting you and making suggestions until you clarify your destination. The same thing applies to good planning. It's a good idea to be clear on the front end about what you are trying to accomplish.

The Beginning – Your starting point is clear. You can't be partially pregnant and you can't get any specific directions from MapQuest if you are unclear about your starting point. Well, maybe I should revise this statement. You can enter an incorrect starting location on MapQuest, but this just reinforces another planning lesson. This produces bogus directions and frustration or failure when you try to execute your trip plan.

The Step-by-Step Instructions – Once again, in the case of pregnancy, Mother Nature takes care of the step-by-step plan. The steps are imbedded in the process. For example, one fairly common interim pregnancy step is morning sickness. Many scientists believe that morning sickness, although inconvenient and miserable, is nature's way of discouraging pregnant women from eating or drinking things that might be toxic to their unborn baby. And, of course, in the case of MapQuest, the Web site does all the work for you and allows you to print step-by-step directions and a map.

In a nutshell, all of this is about one thing ... clarity. The more clarity you have with regard to what you are trying to accomplish, where you are starting, and how you are going to accomplish your plan, the easier it is to execute.

Let's Walk through the Process with One of Your Projects

Step 1 – Define What You Plan to Do

Select a project. Look at the index cards you developed when you read Chapter 1 of this book and identified your 10 highest priorities. Pick one priority, preferably a project that involves several people and a series of tasks that will take a few weeks to complete. If you can easily keep up with what you want to accomplish and the details of how you will accomplish it, you probably do not need a formal project plan. You can use the thinking part of this process and skip the documenting part. Maybe a few notes on a sheet of paper that you can pull out and refer to whenever you decide to work on the project will work fine. For learning this process, select a project that you consider important and a bit complex.

Clarify what you want to accomplish. I know this seems like a dinky step, but it is probably the most important step in the process if you want to avoid frustration and failure. Completing a project is similar to working a jigsaw puzzle. When you begin a jigsaw puzzle you have three options: (1) You can randomly grab the pieces and see if they happen to fit together; (2) You can take all the pieces out of the box, turn them upright and group them according to color, shape, or any other common feature that might help you locate them when you need them; (3) You can study the picture on the front of the box to see how everything should look when the puzzle is complete. Step 3 – studying the picture on the box – is the equivalent of clarifying what you want to accomplish with a project. Doing this first can often save a lot of time and prevent a lot of frustration as the project unfolds.

Here's a quick story I often tell in my training classes to illustrate the value of clarity on the front end of a project. Image I ask you to get "something" for me at the grocery store. This is a very simple project, right? But with only these instructions, it will be a difficult and frustrating task. What if I improve my instructions and ask you to get me "some milk"? Now taking care of the little project will be much easier ... but you can still screw things up since there are many different kinds of milk and sizes of milk containers. Let's try a third time. This time I ask you to get a "gallon of skim milk of a certain brand" and give you all the other details you need to get exactly the kind of milk I want. Now the task is easy. The only difference in request one, two, and three is clarity.

As clarity improves, project execution improves. This seems like one of those "should go without saying" statements. However, lack of clarity is alive and well in the business world. It's a bit strange that people will not tolerate an out-of-focus movie for more than a few seconds. In just a short time, people will be out of their theater seats, shouting and looking for the projectionist or manager. But things can be out of focus for years at work and nobody says a thing.

Keep this simple. If you draw a picture of the end results of your project, what does the picture look like? How can you describe the project, using relatively few words, to someone else (a subordinate who is involved in executing the plan, a boss who must approve it, etc.)?

Step 2 – Define How You Plan to Do It

Clarify how you are going to accomplish what you want to accomplish. Okay, grab a few of those index cards in the pack you opened when you read Chapter 1 and let's discuss a no-frills approach for getting closure on this project.

- Think of one specific, measurable step– any step – you can take to accomplish what you want to accomplish. Hopefully it is logically the first step, but it doesn't have to be.

- On the top of the index card, describe the step in language as clear as the third set of instructions for the trip to the grocery store mentioned previously. Try to use no more than 15 words (or two lines on the card) for your description; less is better, as long as the statement is clear.

- Under the description of the step, write the name of the person primarily responsible for the step. If several people will work on the step, you can put all their names on the card if you'd like. But make sure one, and only one, name is highlighted – the name of the person on the hook for getting the job done … the name of the "go to" person if you need any information or update on the step.

- Finish the card by creating a deadline (or the date of the next check point) for completing the step and recording the date below the name of the person who is responsible for getting it done. At this point, if you are uncertain about a particular date, hold off on this step until later in the process.

Repeat the Process. Now ask: What, if anything, logically comes before or after the step listed on my first card? Answer this question and repeat the previous process of describing the step, naming the owner of the step, and specifying the deadline or check-point date.

Repeat the Process Again. Repeat the process; go forward and backward in terms of the steps you have already planned until you run out of ideas. You do not have to get this perfect on the front end. Don't even try to do that. Do your best, go for excellence, but do not strive for perfection. As the project unfolds and you think of new ideas, you can easily prepare and add other cards ... or toss a card that no longer makes sense. That's how the real world works in terms of project management.

Flip Again. Once you complete your cards, use the flipping-over-index-cards technique we discussed in Chapter 1 to prioritize the steps of the project. Lay all the cards out on your desk. Pick up the card documenting the logical first step and turn it face down. Keep it up until all the cards are in one stack face down. Turn your stack over and you've got your initial plan! If it is easier for you to do so, wait until after this step to determine deadlines or checkpoint dates.

Clarification Meeting. Make copies of the cards (several cards per page since these will be used for discussion purposes) for everyone involved in the project. Gather everyone involved for a 32-minute clarification meeting. Quickly go through the deck of cards and make sure everyone clearly understands their part of the project. Even if you are the only one working on a particular project, it might be a good idea to go through this clarification process with someone not so close to the project to help you confirm that everything looks reasonable.

Step 3 – Do It

Execute Your Plan. Work your cards! Do what you said you would do on your cards when you said you would do them. Use the cards as reminders to monitor the progress of others working on the project. Since each of the cards is labeled with a completion date, they can be placed in your 1 to 31 follow-up files so you can make sure the project is staying on track. As they say, at this point it is "all in the cards!"

If it makes you feel better, you can create a plan document by entering the information on these cards into a spreadsheet. That's up to you.

Try this process with one project. If you think it will help, do the same thing for other projects. I'm not suggesting that you create a documented plan for every little thing you decide to do at work. I am mainly interested in helping you develop productive thinking patterns, or perhaps we can think of this as a design solution, for quickly planning and executing projects. Admittedly, you will probably need to use more sophisticated methods for highly complex projects. But this simple process should work for most of the garden-variety projects you might expect to encounter on a daily basis. Goldilocks would probably like it!

―――――――――――――

For those of you who want a deeper understanding of this planning process, much of it is based on a process explained in *The Path of Least Resistance* written by Robert Fritz. The book is not a strategic planning book, but as it turns out, is one of the best books on planning I have ever encountered.

| 7

The Art and Science of Persuading

Why is a Chapter on Persuasion in this Book?

I decided to include a chapter on persuading others in this book because it is something you must do frequently at work, doing it well is extremely important if you want to be successful, and doing it well can typically help you avoid a lot of busy-work. We've already talked about identifying and prioritizing important things, developing a system for following up on activities, finding things, e-mails, meetings, and projects – activities that are often a part of a typical day. Persuading others is another area for freeing up time and reducing busyness and stress.

To persuade is to convince somebody to do or believe something. You can use the ideas presented in this chapter to persuade audiences of one or audiences of many.

Aristotle was a Persuasive Dude

You might not realize it, but if someone asks how long it takes to get to the nearest beach, you probably formulate your response by using algebra. If I remember correctly, the formula for determining such things is T = D ÷ R, where T is time, D is distance, and R is rate of speed. In my hometown, the D to the beach is 500 miles. It's mostly interstate travel and the speed limit is mostly 70 mph. So, without thinking much about it, I mentally pull up the formula, calculate that 500 divided by 70 is about 7 hours and respond, "Umm, about 7 hours." But what if I didn't understand the basics of math and algebra and I didn't have this little routine imbedded in my mind. This is hard to imagine since I do have it in my mind, but what if I didn't? It would take quite a while longer to come up with an answer to the "how long does it take to get to the beach" question.

It's nice to develop routines similar to algebraic formulas to use when you encounter common life situations. And one situation faced almost every day is figuring out how to persuade somebody to do or believe something. We don't need to reinvent the wheel every time we need to convince somebody of something. We need a "persuading formula" or a mental model of how to go about persuading someone. That leads us to Aristotle.

Apparently in his day, Aristotle was quite a persuasive dude. He was an expert in rhetoric, the art of using language to communicate effectively. Aristotle, in effect, provided us with the algebra of persuasion. Here's the formula: Persuasion = E + L + P where E = Ethos, L = Logos and P = Pathos (Memory tip: If you need *help* with planning a persuasive presentation, drop the "H" from help and remember what the "E," "L," and "P" stand for).

Okay, let's go for a bit more clarity on this ELP thing. Ethos is about the credibility and honesty of the speaker. Logos is about logic, which normally involves using facts and figures to support your topic. Pathos is an appeal to the audience's emotions.

Ethos or "E"

First, what can you do as a communicator to demonstrate ethos, your credibility and the credibility of your message? You can dance around with superficial stuff like dress, grooming, physical positioning, spewing out your credentials and such ... or you can just do your homework. For example, when attempting to persuade somebody (in the absence of a compelling reason not to do so) break your comments into three main points, seven main points, or 10 main points. Think in terms of "the three best reasons to ...," "the seven pitfalls of ...," or "the top 10 ... whatever."

Stick with three whenever possible. The reason is simple; people don't generally need or want to mentally process more than three things in order to make a decision. And the human brain doesn't operate at its best when you overload it with information. If three points can't get the job done, seven or 10 will probably just make things worse. This has to do with what Barry Schwartz calls "choice overload" in his book, *The Paradox of Choice*. And it's much easier to fully develop three points, than seven, 10, or more. Three is a magic number in nature. The number three comes up often in relation to efficiency and effectiveness. It's easy to mentally process three things. Have more than three points and thinking can get fuzzy for most people. You can comprehensively research three points: go deeper, anticipate any potential questions or objections, formulate responses to anticipated questions, and so on.

There will certainly be times when you need to build your case around more than three main points. Perhaps you get a job as a writer for David Letterman's show. However, you are more likely to come off as more focused, organized, knowledgeable, and credible if you stick with three main points.

In general, and especially when attempting to persuade others, it's a good idea to offer your audience what professor Hugh Heclo of George Mason University calls "ordered knowledge." He stated, "The comparative advantage shifts from those with information glut to those with ordered knowledge, from those who can process vast amounts of throughput to those who can explain what is worth knowing and why." I like his thinking!

Logos or "L"

Second, what can you do as a speaker to develop and offer logic supporting your position? Don't overdo this. Gather plenty of facts and figures to support your position, but only use the most compelling facts and figures in your presentation. Here's a fact ... from a personality-wiring point of view, some people base decisions primarily on facts and others base decisions mainly on feelings. The problem ... you never know for sure which approach any particular audience member prefers. Err on the side of using both, some facts and some emotions. Go for balance and quality over quantity. Once again, if you stick with three main points rather than launching into an unplanned, unorganized, blathering, fire-hose approach, gathering facts and figures and persuading people should be much easier.

Pathos or "P"

Third, what can you do to stir the emotions of your audience? Don't overdo this, don't under do it either. You don't have to relate everything to a lost puppy or sick kitty. Just be genuine. Keep it simple. Here are the six major categories of emotions: joy, sadness, anger, fear, disgust, and surprise. Find a way to incorporate brief stories or anecdotes into your presentation that evoke one or more of these emotions. This not only holds people's attention better, it also helps them encode stronger memories of your conversation or presentation.

Back to the Mental Model Concept

The bottom line: Don't reinvent the wheel and start with a head-scratching, anxiety-generating, totally blank canvas when preparing to interact with and persuade someone. Learn a few mental models and you can whip up a pretty persuasive argument in a short time. Here's a step-by-step plan:

1   Hold your fire and take time to plan your comments. Whenever possible, avoid situations where you must spontaneously rise to the occasion and persuade somebody of something. It is perfectly okay in most (but I recognize not all) situations to say, "Let me think about that and get back with you later today." It's not wimpy to have a reputation for getting your thoughts in order before engaging your mouth.

2   Recognize that it is time to "call up" the mental model. Again, don't try to reinvent the wheel each time you need to persuade someone. Learn to recognize when a situation can best be addressed by using a mental model to structure your approach.

3   Clearly define and articulate your position. Let's make this easy. Grab an index card and, in 15 words or less, see if you can state your position, premise, argument, or whatever you prefer to call it on the first two lines of the card. Under the position statement, record your three main supporting points. Don't drag this out. Just do it. You can always improve on your first version later in the process.

4   Prepare more cards. Prepare as many E, L, and P cards as you'd like. When you are finished, pick the most compelling E, L, and P ideas.

5   Ordered knowledge. Lay out the four surviving cards (the one you prepared summarizing your position and your three supporting points, and the surviving cards from you ELP analysis) on your desktop. By now, you know the routine. Flip the last three cards over in the order you plan to present the ideas.

6   Play "Yes, but." You know the "Yes, but" game; no matter how sound your suggestion or argument happens to be, some people always find a way to "Yes, but" you. For example, you might suggest that the sun comes up in the east. Your discussion partner might reply, "Yes, that's usually correct, but what if you are standing on the North Pole during the season when the sun never sets?" "Yes, but" statements are often ridiculous, but they serve a purpose for people who want to knock you off track or try to change the subject. Spend a little time anticipating both excellent and ridiculous "Yes, but" statements and responses.

7   Develop a memory cue for your three main points. For example, if you want to convince someone to try the three modes of persuasion suggested by Aristotle, you might use the letters ELP to represent ethos, logos, and pathos.

8   Practice your delivery.

9   Do it! Okay, we've talked about what to do and how to do it. You can't lose weight by reading a diet book, you can't get in shape by joining a health club, you can't learn to cook by buying a cookbook, and you can't learn to be persuasive by just reading this chapter; sooner or later the rubber has got to hit the road.

This all may seem like much ado about a little thing. However, remember when you learn a pattern and repeat it, you are recruiting new neurons to the learning party. And new neurons at the party mean you can do things much quicker and much better ... two excellent antidotes to the dreaded nemesis we are trying to defeat – busyness. After a few real-world experiences with this model, your brain will reformat some neural pathways and your mind will begin to think and operate this way. You will just do it when the occasion arises, and you may only need to pull out the index cards for special situations.

| 8

Leveraging Your Time Through Networking

Maintaining Meaningful, Mutually Beneficial Relationships

When people hear the word networking they usually think of working a room, mixing and mingling, shaking hands, exchanging business cards, making small talk with strangers, and those sorts of things. That's not the kind of networking I'm talking about. I'm talking about developing a limited number of meaningful, mutually beneficial relationships to help you leverage your time and talent and accomplish much more than you could ever accomplish on your own.

No More Than 24

No matter how good you are at what you do, you will never accomplish more than a fraction of your potential until you overcome the limitations of a 24-hour day and realize it's time to stop trying to do everything on your own. In the book *Tribal Leadership* by Dave Logan, John King, and Halee Fischer-Wright, the authors reveal the results of a rigorous eight-year study of approximately 24,000 people in more than two dozen organizations and lay out five stages in terms of creating a productive, meaningful life. Stage three members, also referred to as Lone Warriors, are those primarily focused on their *individual* performance and accomplishments. Here's an interesting point they make about Lone Warriors:

"No matter how hard they work, they can't punch through the barrier of a day that has only twenty-four hours. They've hit the point of diminishing returns, so the harder they work, the less effective they are, and the less their efforts seem to matter."

There seems to be only one logical way to overcome this personal limitation. You must accept that stellar performance emerges not from individual performance, but from networks of meaningful and mutually beneficial relationships.

It's simple. Get more done with your 24 hours by bartering and leveraging your time. Take care of the people in your network and they will take care of you. This does not have to be a time-consuming process, but it will save significant time in the long run. You don't need to include a lot of people in your network. You just need to include people who have the knowledge and skills that complement your talents, people you trust and respect, and people who feel the same way about you.

How Many Make a Network?

Rather than executing a quantity-based networking strategy, focus on executing a quality-based strategy. Let's make this easy. Rather than trying to maintain relationships with hundreds of people that you think might be willing and able to help you, develop and maintain high quality relationships with 20 people that you know are willing and able to help you. Agree to help each other, determine specifically how you can help each other, and establish a specific plan for staying strongly connected.

The Plan

Let's cut to the chase and get to the step-by-step plan so you can master this critical workplace function – leveraging your time.

1   Get your networking attitude in order. As David E. Kelley suggests in his excellent book *How to Be a Star at Work,* develop the attitude that knowledge is not a public resource and access to highly knowledgeable people is not a basic right; it is a privilege that must be earned. In any given organization, some people's phone messages are quickly returned or their calls are taken in the first place,

some people's requests for help are granted quickly, and some people are put off or ignored ... forever! Get your mind right!

2   Identify your bartering skill. Establish some kind of expertise that will be of value to others to use as your bartering resource. This will allow you to earn the privilege of gaining access to other high performers. For example, years ago I chose public speaking as my bartering chip. I learned a lot about the process of public speaking, including designing a presentation, delivering a presentation, and so on. Most people dread or fear public speaking. So I am often called on to help develop a presentation, provide coaching tips for delivery, or to speak to someone's group.

Be creative. Identify and develop your unique bartering resource. Become so good at whatever you choose that if anyone asks, "Who can help me with this?" everybody, I mean everybody, points to you! If you can't come up with something quickly, be patient. Listen to people's complaints. It's fun to be really good at something that most people dread or complain about. Select a pervasive complaint and quietly become an expert at handling it. Or use reverse thinking and listen to your co-workers' dreams and aspirations. What can you learn that a lot of people want to do or know about? For example, Kelley's book relates a story about a young research scientist who discovered that her more seasoned co-workers, who paid little attention to her at the time, were not using the latest statistical tools. She used these statistical methods to develop a solution that had eluded her co-workers. Bingo! Suddenly, everybody wanted her help.

Okay, so you're trying to eliminate busyness and now you have more people who want your time. Isn't that going to make things worse? Remember, these should be mutually beneficial relationships. As you become better known for your bartering expertise and continue to nurture your network, you'll have access to experts in other areas to help you when the needs arise.

Here are a few examples of potential bartering-chip skills:

– Analyzing data/troubleshooting
– Computer/software expertise
– Communication/speaking/presentations
– Networking
– Creative thinking
– Negotiating
– Writing
– Video production
– Math and statistics
– Human relations (e.g. mentoring, coaching, conflict resolution)
– Sales and persuasion
– Project organization and management
– Editing, punctuation, and grammar

- Any highly technical skill related to your field of expertise
- Any important area of knowledge related to your field of expertise

3. Identify trading partners. Start simple and identify a handful of partners to get your network started. You can expand your network at any time, but for now, think about potential areas of expertise you may need help with in the future and identify potential bartering partners. You should always be willing to give first in these relationships and genuinely be willing to give more than you expect in return. Consider people both in and outside your organization, as well as those who don't run in the same circles as you, since these connections often provide excellent ties to other people totally outside your current circle of influence. For starters, consider the following:

- *A highly credible connector.* Some people are naturally fond of connecting with others. They love to network and hundreds of people are within their circle of influence. If you get in their good graces, they will serve as your connection to the vast number of people in their network.

- *A vocal advocate.* Some people love to share their experiences. If they go to a nice restaurant, see a good movie, or read a good book, they want to tell everybody about their experience. These are also great people to have in your network due to the leveraging potential of knowing them. If you convince them of something, you are potentially convincing many others. But be careful. They also willingly share bad experiences, so treat these relationships with care.

- *A technology expert.* Unfortunately, work activity often comes to a grinding halt when technology decides to misbehave. It's nice to get your request for assistance placed at or near the front of the line. Add a technology expert to your network and you can potentially save vast amounts of time by pushing through the technology downtime more quickly.

- *A speaking/presentation expert.* Sooner or later, if you are a high achiever, you are going to have to get up in front of a group of people and communicate your ideas. Who will you turn to for help if the presentation is critically important?

- *A highly creative person.* Who is the most creative person you know? Add him or her to your list of networking partners. Your creative partner can help you think through challenging situations and come up with innovative ideas. Many years ago I watched a video about Apple computer (long before they were iCool). The narrator talked about innovation being at the edge of things. That's where most new discoveries are made, he said. That's where amazing things get done. If you stay "down the middle" and never get out on the edge, all you can hope for in life is "better sameness, and who wants that?"

- *Knowledge experts in fields directly related to your intellectual and professional growth.* What areas of knowledge do you need to pursue on an ongoing basis to master your chosen profession? Who do you know that is intellectually and professionally farther down the road than you? Who can accelerate your journey?

For example, my chosen field relates to the behavioral aspects of workplace productivity. It became clear that it would be beneficial to know experts in psychology, psychiatry, neurology, anthropology, and many other fields related to human behavior. I am now extremely grateful that if I need help understanding a concept, I have experts in my network who I can call. I recently wanted to know more about a particular form of dysfunctional behavior. My choices were to read several books and articles on the topic and try to figure it out on my own, or call my expert friend with over 30 years of practical experience related to the topic. In a brief phone call he explained the basics and recommended the best book on the topic. I read the book, he was right! I cannot imagine how much time and effort this relationship saved me.

Think about your chosen profession. Maybe you need experts in jet engine mechanics, biology, philosophy, video production, butchering, baking, or candlestick making. Pick the experts that will best fit your dream-team network.

4. Do your homework. Study your network partners. Learn as much as you can about their work and personal interests. Knowing the names of their spouses, significant others, kids, and other important facts is probably a good idea. Never meet with them or call them unprepared. If you are asking for their help, summarize what you want to accomplish or the problem you are trying to solve. Go into the meeting with well thought-out questions. Do not waste the time of your networking partners! If they are experts, many people are probably seeking their help. Get your act together before you ask them for help.

5. Begin nurturing your network. Add more members to your network as you think of them or encounter candidates in your day-to-day activities, but keep your total number of network partners to a reasonably low number. These are not casual contacts. These are people with whom you are going to develop meaningful, mutually beneficial relationships. This will take a structured, ongoing, proactive effort.

The worst time to begin building your network is when you need it. Get your network in place now and start giving to your partners long before you need to be on the receiving end. Here are some examples of things you can do:

- Help your network partners accomplish goals that are important to them (meet a prospect, make a sale, solve a problem, prepare a presentation, etc.). Ask, "What is important to you and how can I help you accomplish it?"

- Help your network partners build and strengthen their networks.

- Be a valuable resource for your network partners (send or refer them to articles or books relevant to their work or personal interests).

- Plan personal interactions with your network partners (lunch, coffee, beers, etc.).

- Keep in touch with your network partners when you do not need them with occasional phone calls, e-mails, or personal notes. Not enough to be intrusive, just enough to maintain the relationships.

- Let your network partners know they are important to you. Be creative. One of my business colleagues sends me a note every time the cost of stamps increases along with a dozen or so one-cent stamps. I'm reminded of their thoughtful gesture each time I use these one-cent stamps.

6 Give your network partners credit when credit is due. Recognize the contributions your partners make to your success both privately and publicly.

This is an important part of building these valuable partnerships.

Okay, we've talked about what to do and how to do it. Now get going ... do it! Make it easy on yourself. Put 10 names on 10 index cards and do at least one thing a day to nurture at least one of your network partner relationships. After you get the hang of it, work up to about 20 partners. That way you can get in the habit of improving one partnership every working day of the month. Leverage your time and talent through networking.

| 9

Busy Tapes

A Tough Question to Answer: What's Normal?

On the surface, busyness is not necessarily bad. Maybe it is, maybe it isn't. Being busy is a normal part of most people's lives ... until it becomes excessive. Then it's no longer normal. But that brings up another question: What is excessive in relation to busyness? The best way to determine if busyness has crossed the line and morphed into excessive, self-defeating, or dysfunctional behavior is to consider the following factors:

- Frequency
- Duration
- Intensity
- Negative Impact

I doubt it, but busyness might actually help you increase your productivity in the short run. However, staying busy all the time (frequency), for too long a period of time (duration), while demanding a high level of energy (intensity), can easily lead to health problems, unhappiness, relationship problems, burnout, and other unfavorable consequences (negatively impacting some area of your life).

If you're having trouble determining if you've crossed over to excessive busyness, you might want to ask a close friend or confidant to help you evaluate your own behavior. No matter how weird we behave, we are all pretty much wired to think, "Why isn't everybody normal like me?" In other words, your excessive behavior might feel normal.

We've covered several mechanical-like solutions to the problem of excessive busyness: getting better at prioritizing and staying focused on important issues, getting better at handling incoming demands on your time and energy, improving your e-mail processing skills, and others. But what if these solutions aren't enough to solve your busyness problem? What if there's something else causing you to over-schedule, over-commit, and over-work your days? Let's take a quick look at one potential factor we haven't discussed – the busyness X factor.

The X Factor of Busyness

X factor is an expression referring to an indefinable quality, particularly when referring to an individual's behavior, personality, and success (or lack thereof).

Exploring the X factor of busyness – the intangible, hard-to-define element that influences our behavior – leads to what I refer to as busyness tapes.

Some therapists call the intangibles that influence our behavior psychological tapes, or tapes, because they work like old-fashion computer programs. Not that long ago, computers were programmed with punched paper tapes – long strips of paper in which holes were punched to store data. The data was encoded by the presence or absence of holes. A computer performed certain functions, or behaved in a certain way, by reading these tapes. The actions of the computer were, in effect, controlled by these tapes.

Psychological tapes work in a similar way. In your brain, memories perform the function that punched tapes performed in the old days with computers. Your experiences are encoded as memories and these memories, in turn, serve as computer-like programs that influence and control your behavior.

But human beings are more complicated than computers. We actually have two separate memory encoding systems. Psychological tapes are more like two-track video camera tapes used to record video and sound. One memory system records the facts related to an experience and the other system records the feelings associated with the facts. These two components are merged as they are encoded and stored in our brain. That's why when something triggers any facts related to an old memory, the feelings associated with the memory also resurface.

So, what does all this have to do with busyness? Well, some of us have memories related to someone in a position of authority trying to keep us busy, or the correlated psychological opposite ... trying to keep us from being lazy! Who knows, maybe your parents laid a guilt trip on you when you were hanging around doing nothing. Maybe you deserved it, maybe not. The point is that at an early age, you may have begun to associate guilt with idleness. If you received enough of this "programming," this guilt/idleness association may have become an influential aspect of your adult personality – an X factor.

Why is This Important?

All this psychological stuff might seem a bit touchy-feely, but this is likely the real culprit! This X factor is often the common cause of excessive busyness. Babies don't typically come into the world wired to work 14-hour days. They don't overload their day, over-commit, or choose to remain tethered to energy-sucking gadgets 24/7. We learn to do this! That's the bad news. The good news, according to what we now know about the process of neuroplasticity and rewiring our brains, is that what was learned can be unlearned.

A Personal Confession

I am personally a recovering workaholic. I've been through the unproductive, busyness, stress-inducing mode of operating, worked through it, and emerged on the other side. That's my crucible – "my situation in which concentrated forces interact to cause or influence change or development," according to *Merriam Webster*. I have been in remission for over 25 years, so some of my new friends (who know little about the younger version of me) probably will laugh at this admission. In terms of work, I have been living on island-time for at least 10 years. Once I discovered and processed my busyness tapes, I reversed course and chose uber-laid-backness as my ongoing career strategy. Not surprisingly (considering what I have learned about workplace productivity over the last few decades), I get much more accomplished with this strategy.

Discovering Your Busyness X Factor

Here's a simple exercise to help uncover any tapes or other beliefs that might be causing your excessive busyness:

1   Divide and prepare to explore. Divide your current age by five and round up. For example, if you are 43 years old, the answer is nine. If you are 57, the answer is 12. Get that many sheets of paper. Nope, we are not going to use index cards for this. I want you to have more room to write or draw things. Label the sheets of paper consecutively in the following manner: Birth to 5, 6 to 10, 11 to 15, 16 to 20, and so forth and so on up to your current age.

2   Random thoughts. Take one sheet at a time (start at birth and go forward) and record your thoughts – good, bad, and ugly – related to two things:

   – Who were the most influential people in your life during that period of time?

   – What were the most influential experiences in your life during that period of time?

   Don't over-think this! Stay mentally loose and stay mentally random. If you have moved on to another five-year period and think of something that belongs on another sheet, go back and jot it down. Use keywords, notes, doodles, or whatever you feel like to record your thoughts. At this point, don't try to analyze or evaluate. That's the next step.

3   Look for tapes and beliefs. After you finish the last page, go back and look over your notes and drawings. Some other interesting stuff might come up. That's okay. Try to focus mainly on people and experiences that created psychological tapes that might be influencing your tendency to overload yourself, work long hours, and so on. As they say, this ain't rocket science. My dad is still living and will probably read this book. He is an absolute great parent. But damn, I wish he would have eased up on his Saturday morning ritual during my, oh so important and delicate, formative years. This was the typical Saturday morning drill:

Him: Get up son!
Me: Aww Daddy ... leave me alone, it's early.
Him: Get up and get busy!
Me: What for?
Him: What? Are you planning to stay in bed all day?
Me: No, but it's early. And it's Saturday!
Him: Get up and get busy!
Me: Why? I don't have anything to do!
Him: Then I'll find something for you to do!

Looking back, it's all pretty funny. But later in life I had a pretty strong "stay busy" tape. And for some unknown reason, I would typically try to wash and wax the paint off the cars, cut the grass whether it needed it or not, and generally stay incredibly busy with chores all day every Saturday. Or I would go into the office and work all day.

Here are a few things to consider as you think through the people and events of your past:

- Look for influences that might be causing you to believe your value as a human being is somehow attached to, or a function of, your level of work activity or job responsibility, for example, the belief that the busier you are the more important you are. This premise is commonly accepted, but totally false. Check out *The Six Pillars of Self-Esteem* by Nathaniel Branden if this is something you want to further explore.

- Look for situations where, for whatever reason, you were strongly praised or rewarded for being a high achiever or highly active. Probably by a significant authority figure in your life at the time (parent, caregiver, teacher, or coach).

- Look for situations where, for whatever reason, you were strongly criticized or punished for being extremely lazy. Probably by a significant authority figure in your life at the time (parent, caregiver, teacher, or coach).

- You get the idea. Look for experiences or people who might be seeds, or nurturers, of your busyness X factor.

Rewriting Tapes

If you are struggling with busyness tapes, there is great value in just knowing and understanding the origins of your busyness. In many cases, knowing and understanding is the fix. Some of the issues literally melt away on their own when you discover and understand the underlying tape. A book titled *It's Not as Bad as It Seems* by Ed Nottingham is also a great resource to help deal with some of these issues. But if you uncover something that is genuinely disturbing to you, seek professional help.

You can also develop a tape rewriting process. Once I zero in on a tape I no longer want to nurture, I perform a three-part ritual loosely based on my version of a form of therapy called transactional analysis:

1. I get in a childlike (not to be confused with childish) frame of mind and ask myself, "What do I really want to do?" In the case of the busyness tape created by my Saturday morning childhood ritual, I might ask myself, "Do I really want to get up and do chores all day?" It is very important that you remain in the childlike frame of mind when you answer the question. In this case I responded, "Nope ... don't wanna ... ain't gonna do it ... nooooooooway José!"

2. Next, I get serious and consider the consequences of my choice. In this case, I realize that life will go on quite nicely if I sleep a bit longer.

3. After considering the consequences of my choice, and if I am still okay with my decision, I do it! I do what the child-like me really wants to do. The old tape may resurface and try to rain on my parade. But I repeat the following pre-rehearsed statement, "How bizarre is that! I am still letting my parents control my behavior at my age!" This is phrased as a statement not a question. And then, in the case of the Saturday morning tape ... I do it! I sleep in if I feel like it!

Have fun exploring your busyness tapes! Get rid of them if they are no longer serving you well.

| 10

Following Through

Increasing the Odds That You Will Follow Through

We are down to the last chapter. It's time to address one more extremely important issue related to increasing productivity and happiness. Hopefully by now, you've put some design solutions in place to help you enjoy a more balanced and productive work life. Now it's time to talk about a long-term plan for following through and maintaining reasonable order in your life – reasonable order because it is not realistic or necessarily desirable to try and over-structure your days and eliminate the positive experiences that are sometimes created by flexibility and uncertainty.

I do not have to tell you that human beings do not always follow through with their intentions. You already know this quite well ... especially if you have a teenager. But do you know why? According to Dr. Steve Levinson, author of the book *Following Through*, a design flaw in the human brain is one of the main culprits. Since I read his book, I've had several interesting conversations with Steve about the fact that the brain is not designed to follow through with many of our modern-day intentions. Your brain is designed to follow through with many primitive intentions ... hunger, thirst, sex, running from a saber-toothed tiger, and other such activities. But it is not designed to get up early and catch a plane, multitask, work long hours, and that sort of thing.

For example, if you need to get up early tomorrow morning to catch a flight, will you rely solely on your intentions to wake up on time? Probably not. Most of us will rely on what Steve calls a cueing device to bridge the gap between our intentions and actions – something to cue our memory and make sure we follow through and get up on time. And the use of cueing devices is quite easy. In this case, the cueing device will probably be some sort of garden-variety alarm clock.

What's the Problem?

Here's the basic problem. We do have some built-in cueing devices to take care of certain priorities such as eating, sleeping, thirst, and so on. But we do not have built-in cueing devices to remind us to follow through on things like work-related priorities we want to accomplish.

Another aspect of the problem is that we are all too brainy. We don't just have one brain. We have several brains (all residing in the same 3-pound, grapefruit-size, wrinkled biological mass of tissue) that fight for control of our behavior. Just the other day I was driving near the venue of a major sporting event. At one intersection several cops were directing traffic. When I pulled up to the intersection, one cop put his hand out sternly directing me to stop and another was waving vigorously at me to proceed and get out of the way. That's how the brain works sometimes.

In terms of a workplace example, one area of your brain might be telling you to work on an important project today and avoid putting it off until the last minute. But another area of your brain might be telling you to Web-surf, check e-mails, or go join the folks in the break room for birthday cake. According to Steve, there is no built-in biological mechanism to coordinate and reconcile the conflicting desires of the different brain areas. And here's a key issue. The area of the brain that is most involved in directing methodical behavior and controlling impulsive behavior is significantly inhibited or shut down when you are busy, in a hurry, and under stress. In these situations, the part of the brain that likes to eat several donuts at a time, wolf down an entire bowl of M&Ms, watch mindless sitcoms on television, and procrastinate is in charge.

The Solution

Steve outlines many potential solutions in his book. One of my personal favorites is spotlighting. Spotlighting is based on the premise that whatever you think about expands and becomes more important and prominent in your life. Spotlighting is a way to increase your focus on important goals and make sure they remain top-of-mind issues.

Years ago, when I was in college, we were required to watch a driver's education film distributed by the Ohio State Highway Patrol called *Signal 30* before leaving campus for spring break. Signal 30 is radio code cop-speak for death on the highway. Man that video was disturbing! It was all about fatal car accidents on the highways of Ohio. It graphically showed mangled, and sometimes burned, vehicles and bodies. After watching the video, my clear intention was to drive safely forever! And it worked for a few days. Driving safely was definitely on the top of my mind for about three days ... and then it faded. I still intellectually intended to drive cautiously, but I slacked off significantly in terms of follow through as the memories of the video faded.

If follow through fades in these kinds of circumstances, imagine how easily it fades when intentions are related to paperwork, work projects, keeping up with e-mails, filing things, or conducting effective and efficient meetings. So, I want to wrap this book up by suggesting a spotlighting exercise to help you keep the ideas you have read and learned top-of-mind until you convert them into habitual behavior.

According to Steve, spotlighting involves three simple steps:

1 Clearly articulate what you intend to do.

2 Create a reminder, a cue, which stimulates you to follow up on your planned actions.

3 Find a way to make sure you'll be exposed to the cue on a regular basis until you convert your intellectual intentions into habitual behavior.

Spotlighting Your Way to the Good Life!

Spotlighting can be used to develop a variety of habits related to different areas of your life. But for now, let's set up a spotlighting strategy to help you focus on the overall goal of replacing frantic motion with constructive action. Then, all the benefits we have talked about should fall into place on their own – reduced busyness and stress, increased productivity, increased happiness and fulfillment, and a balanced lifestyle.

1 Create a brief statement articulating your vision of success with regard to your ongoing lifestyle at work. Be specific. Remember the puzzle example earlier in the book? Clearly define the picture on the cover of the box. Keep it simple and easy to remember. It is fine to refer to a written statement when your cueing device prompts you to think of your vision, but it would be better to know it by heart.

2 Get a cueing device. Find something to periodically prompt you to think of your vision statement. You

can set an alarm on your phone or computer; you can use a kitchen timer, an alarm clock, or anything that works for you. I highly recommend you consider a cueing device called the MotivAider created by Dr. Levinson. It's designed to help transform intentions into action, and as far as I know, the only device available specifically designed to help people change habits. It's not expensive, and a discount is available to our readers when you place your order at www.dmetraining.com. You can set it to prompt you every five minutes, 32 minutes, 67 minutes, or any time interval up to 24 hours. It vibrates silently so it works great in an office environment.

3   Set up a cueing routine. In the beginning, I suggest you set your cueing device for every 32 minutes. After a few days, use your judgment to extend the time intervals until you no longer need to spotlight your intentions.

If you feel you need to do more than just generally think of your overall vision, consider pausing a few minutes when your cueing device prompts you, think of your intentions, and then glance at the following checklist:

- Have I prepared and prioritized my 10 index cards for the day and set aside time to work on at least my top three priorities?

- Have I set up my follow-up files and am I doing a reasonable job of creating reminders for important activities and checking my files on a regular basis?

- Have I set up my reference filing system and am I doing a reasonable job of filing items so I can find them when I need them?

- Have I performed e-mail triage today?

- Am I doing a good job of making the most of any meetings I conduct or attend?

- Am I staying on top of any significant tasks related to projects I am involved with or responsible for?

- Am I consistently using and improving my mental model for persuading others?

- Am I doing things to develop and improve my bartering network?

- Am I continuing to identify and rewrite psychological tapes that drive self-defeating behavior?

- Am I using a structured process for following through with my intentions?

Success!

Keep one thought in mind as you implement the ideas in this book ... nothing in this book is hard to do. It will be best if you implement these ideas over a period of 10 consecutive working days. However, as a practical matter, implement the ideas presented here over whatever timeframe works best for you, given what is going on in your life at this time.

One of the few downsides of becoming highly focused, organized, and productive is that you begin to feel like a character in *The Odd Couple*. For those of you too young to remember, *The Odd Couple* is an award winning Neil Simon play (also film and television series) about two roommates. One is a fastidious neat freak; the other is a poker playing, cigar smoking slob. The neurotic Felix was constantly harping at the slovenly Oscar to clean up his act. Don't become a Felix in an office of Oscars. If you want to maintain any hope of influencing those around you, you will be better off following the advice of Edgar Guest in his poem *The Sermon*:

> I'd rather see a sermon, than hear one any day.
> I'd rather you walk with me, than merely show the way.
> For the lessons you deliver, may be very wise and true,
> but I think I'll get my lessons, by observing what you do.
> I might misunderstand all this high advice you give,
> but I won't misunderstand how you act and how you live.

You will realize significant synergistic benefits if you implement these ideas along with a partner or group of coworkers. Be a role model to those around you and encourage them to also choose constructive action over frantic motion.

Thank you for choosing to spend some time with me. I am honored to share these thoughts with you and hope these ideas help you accomplish your personal goals and dreams ... whatever they may be! I wish you much success!

About the Author

Chris Crouch has an impressive background in sales, sales management, training, and as an executive for a Fortune 500 company. However, his passion has always been reading, learning, and teaching. Among other topics, he has spent years researching and studying both the mental and physical aspects of living a more joyful and productive life. His goal is to find simple, easy-to-implement ideas that work in the real world.

Chris regularly writes, speaks, and teaches on topics related to workplace productivity. He is president and founder of DME Training and Consulting, author of several books, and the developer of the GO System training course. He currently lives with his wife in Memphis, Tenn.

Chris is always looking for ideas to improve productivity. If you have techniques that work for you and are willing to share them with him, or if you would like to discuss any of the ideas presented in this book, please write to him at cc@dmetraining.com.